PICNICS

FABULOUS FOOD FOR OUTDOOR FEASTS

PICNICS

FABULOUS FOOD FOR OUTDOOR FEASTS

LOUISE PICKFORD ≈ PHOTOGRAPHS BY MARIE-LOUISE AVERY

a Salamander book

Published by Salamander Books Limited
LONDON • NEW YORK

© 1992 Salamander Books Limited
129-137 York Way
London N7 9LG
United Kingdom

ISBN 0 86101 641 6

Distributed in the UK by
Hodder & Stoughton Services
P.O. Box 6, Mill Road
Dunton Green, Sevenoaks,
Kent TN13 2XX

All correspondence concerning the content
of this volume should be addressed to
Salamander Books Ltd.

CREDITS

Editor: ANNE MCDOWALL
Designer: TIM SCOTT
Photographer: MARIE-LOUISE AVERY
Home Economist: LOUISE PICKFORD
Stylist: LUCY ELWORTHY
Illustrator: ORIOL BATH
Typesetting: SX COMPOSING LTD.
Colour reproduction: SCANTRANS PTE. LTD.
Printed in Singapore

CONTENTS

~

INTRODUCTION

The pleasure of eating 'al fresco' is something that has been enjoyed for centuries. There is little doubt that food simply tastes better when eaten in the open air – it is magical – the flavours of the food seem more intense and the atmosphere more relaxed. This book aims to satisfy all those who enjoy eating outdoors, whether having a picnic, a barbecue, or a dinner party in the garden.

A picnic will vary depending on the occasion: it may be a spontaneous event, where the most important thing is just to be outside on a balmy summer's day; or a more grand occasion, needing more planning and preparation. Whichever, it's the fun of eating 'al fresco' that really counts.

Picnics to Go, the first chapter in the book, provides recipes for the spur-of-the-moment picnic, proving that it's possible to prepare more than just a soggy sandwich and still make a quick get-away. Moveable feasts, on the other hand, offers a selection of more elaborate recipes, when you have time to plan and prepare the dishes.

Barbecues, by their very nature, require a little more organization, but in the chapter Food with Fire, there is a good cross-section of recipes to choose from that are suitable for any such occasion. Because much of the food is served hot, a barbecue is not restricted to summer days, but is also ideal for autumn evenings.

Of course, there are times when you will want to eat outdoors when you will still have easy access to the kitchen. The final chapter, Dining Alfresco, contains the most elaborate dishes, but even these have been devised so that you need spend as little time in the kitchen as possible, allowing you more time to devote to your guests.

There are several practicalities that need to be considered when planning an alfresco meal of any kind.

Packaging of food Picnic hampers are the most obvious and ideal containers for the food to be packed into, but they are by no means a necessity. If you have one, fine, but if not, a large basket or box will suffice. Pack dishes tightly into the box or basket to stop them moving around and becoming damaged on the way to the picnic, and always pack the most durable items at the bottom.

Food safety The one essential item for any meal to be eaten outside on a hot day is a cool box (with reusable plastic ice packs). Use this to transport and store foods that may spoil if left out in the heat. A large thermos flask is also very useful to keep soups or sauces hot (and can also be used to keep things cold) until required.

Last-minute preparations Just before setting out for your picnic or barbecue, check your basket or hamper to make sure that you have packed everything you need. Finding that you have no cork screw or cutlery once you arrive in the middle of nowhere will be extremely frustrating. Don't forget to take along a large plastic bag to pick up all the rubbish at the end of the meal.

Notes on ingredients

1 tbsp chopped fresh herbs = 1 tsp dried herbs
Pepper should be freshly ground unless otherwise stated
Always use a good-quality olive oil

All recipes serve 6 unless otherwise stated.

PICNICS TO GO

For picnic-lovers everywhere there can be no greater inspiration to get up and go out than awakening to a glorious sunny morning. The recipes in this first chapter have been devised specifically to help you prepare a picnic in as little time as possible, so as to enjoy the day at its best. They are not only quick and easy to assemble, but use staple ingredients that, in general, can be found in most store cupboards or 'fridges, and fresh foods that you should be able to obtain from your local store. Easily obtainable alternatives are given for any ingredients that may be harder to find.

As a quick get-away is the order of the day, most of the recipes can be prepared within half an hour and tips are often given in head-notes for the most suitable method of packaging and transportation.

(Plastic and paper tableware are ideal for serving the food on a spontaneous picnic, as they are easy to pack into a hamper or basket, with no fear of breakages.)

It is not only the picnicker who will benefit and make use of the recipes in this section, but also the ardent walker or perhaps an outdoor worker. Both need to make an early start and these dishes are ideal, as they can be easily packed away into a ruck sack or back pack. Whatever the occasion, a few minutes' planning before you start will ensure that you have a successful and enjoyable meal.

CONTENTS

CHILLED MELON & MINT SOUP

~

If you have room in your picnic hamper, take along the hollowed-out melon shells. They make excellent and attractive soup bowls.

═══

6 SMALL CHARENTAIS OR CANTALOUPE MELONS

2 SPRING ONIONS, TRIMMED AND CHOPPED

2 TBSP/30 ML CHOPPED MINT

4 TBSP/60 ML WHITE WINE

¾ TSP/3.75 ML GROUND GINGER

¾ PINT/450 ML GREEK YOGURT

SALT AND PEPPER

TO GARNISH

MINT SPRIGS

═══

◇ Slice the tops from the melons and reserve. Scoop out the seeds into a sieve over a bowl to catch the juices. Discard the seeds but reserve the juice.
◇ Scoop out the melon flesh and purée with the spring onion, mint, wine and ginger in a food processor or blender. Stir in the yogurt and up to ½ pint/300 ml of reserved juice. Season to taste.
◇ Pour into a plastic container and chill until required.
◇ Transport the soup in the container, in a cool box, and serve chilled in the melon shells, if wished. Garnish with mint sprigs.

SUMMER AVOCADO DIP WITH CRUDITÉS

~

This is a fresh-tasting avocado dip with cottage cheese, mint and just enough lemon juice to add a light tang. Cover the surface of the dip with cling film to prevent the avocado from discolouring.

═══

1 LARGE RIPE AVOCADO

1 TBSP/15 ML LEMON JUICE

2 TBSP/30ML CHOPPED FRESH MINT

3 OZ/75 G COTTAGE CHEESE

1 SMALL RED PEPPER, DE-SEEDED AND FINELY CHOPPED

SALT AND PEPPER

CRUDITÉS

FENNEL, LEEKS, LETTUCE HEARTS, RADISHES, TOMATOES, BLACK AND GREEN GRAPES

═══

◇ Halve and peel the avocado, discarding the stone. Chop the flesh and purée in a food processor or blender with the lemon juice and mint until smooth and creamy.
◇ Transfer to a small bowl and stir in the cheese and pepper and season to taste.
◇ Cover with cling film and then top with foil or a tight-fitting lid and keep cool until required.
◇ Serve the dip with a selection of crudités.

LEFT *Chilled melon and mint soup*
RIGHT *Summer avocado dip with crudités*

SMOKED SALMON 'SAUSAGES'

~

A mixture of salmon, prawns and curd cheese is rolled up in rectangles of smoked salmon to form sausage-shaped parcels.

---

8 OZ/225 G SMOKED SALMON

FILLING

4 OZ/100 G PEELED PRAWNS

2 OZ/50 G CURD CHEESE

3 SPRING ONIONS, TRIMMED

1 SMALL CLOVE GARLIC, CRUSHED

GRATED RIND OF 1 LIME

PINCH OF GRATED NUTMEG

SALT AND PEPPER

◇ Carefully remove the cellophane from between the layers of salmon and cut the strips into 6 rectangles, 3×4 in/7.5×10 cm, overlapping them if necessary.
◇ Finely chop the smoked salmon trimmings.
◇ Place all the remaining ingredients in a food processor and purée until smooth. Transfer to a bowl and stir in the chopped salmon.
◇ Place ⅙th of the mixture along 1 narrow edge of each smoked salmon rectangle, and roll up to form a sausage shape. Wrap up each sausage individually in cling film and twist the ends to seal the filling.
◇ Chill until required, transport in a cool box and serve sliced, with crusty bread, crisp biscuits or a salad.

ICED CUCUMBER SOUP

~

For the best result serve this soup as chilled as possible, preferably adding a few ice cubes at the last minute.

---

3 LARGE CUCUMBERS

9 SPRING ONIONS, TRIMMED AND CHOPPED

1 TBSP/15 ML CHOPPED FRESH DILL

2 CARTONS MUSTARD AND CRESS

JUICE OF 1 LEMON

2 TBSP/30 ML OLIVE OIL

½ PINT/300 ML NATURAL YOGURT

¼ PINT/150 ML SINGLE CREAM

TO SERVE

ICE CUBES (OPTIONAL)

MUSTARD AND CRESS

◇ Peel and de-seed the cucumbers and cut them into thick slices.
◇ Place in a food processor or blender, with all the remaining ingredients and blend until smooth.
◇ Chill in the coolest part of the refrigerator and transfer to a thermos flask just before required.
◇ Add a couple of ice cubes and mustard and cress to each serving, if wished.

TOP LEFT *Smoked salmon 'sausages'*
BOTTOM RIGHT *Iced cucumber soup*

CURRIED EGGS

~

This is a delicious and attractive way to serve hard-boiled eggs. A curried mayonnaise sauce is poured over halved eggs, and sprinkled with a little sieved egg yolk. The eggs, sauce and garnish should be transported separately, and put together just before serving.

3 TBSP/45 ML OLIVE OIL

1 SMALL ONION, CHOPPED

1 CLOVE GARLIC, CHOPPED

1 TSP/5 ML GRATED FRESH ROOT GINGER

1 TBSP/15 ML CURRY POWDER

7 FLOZ/200 ML READY-MADE MAYONNAISE

3 FLOZ/75 ML NATURAL YOGURT

1 TBSP/15 ML LEMON JUICE

1 TBSP/15 ML CHOPPED FRESH CORIANDER OR PARSLEY

4 SPRING ONIONS, TRIMMED AND CHOPPED

12 HARD-BOILED EGGS, PEELED

SALT AND PEPPER

TO GARNISH

CORIANDER SPRIGS (OPTIONAL)

◇ Heat the oil and sauté the onion, garlic, ginger and curry powder for 5 minutes. Strain the oil through a fine sieve into a bowl and leave to cool slightly.
◇ Stir in all the remaining ingredients except for the eggs and season to taste.
◇ Cut 9 of the eggs in half and arrange, cut side down, on a large deep-lipped plate, or shallow dish. Cover with cling film and set aside.
◇ Finely chop the remaining eggs, except the yolk of one, and stir into the mayonnaise mixture. Place in a dish with a tight-fitting lid, and chill until ready to transport.
◇ Sieve the remaining yolk and transfer to a screw-top jar. Transport the 3 containers separately.
◇ Spoon over the sauce and garnish with the sieved yolk and coriander sprigs. Serve with wholemeal bread.

AUBERGINE PÂTÉ

~

This makes a delicious vegetarian spread or dip.

1 LARGE AUBERGINE

1 SMALL CLOVE GARLIC, CRUSHED

1 TBSP/15 ML CHOPPED FRESH CORIANDER OR 1 TSP/5 ML GROUND CORIANDER SEEDS

1 TBSP/15 ML LEMON JUICE

2 TSP/10 ML TAHINI PASTE

¼ TSP/1.25 ML GROUND CUMIN

1 TBSP/15 ML OLIVE OIL

SALT AND PEPPER

◇ Heat the oven to 200°C/400°F/gas mark 6. Prick the aubergine all over with the point of a sharp knife and bake for 30 minutes, until the skin is wrinkled and the flesh feels soft. Remove from the oven and leave to cool for 10 minutes.
◇ Peel and discard the skin and chop the flesh.
◇ Place in a food processor or blender with all the remaining ingredients and blend until smooth.
◇ Transfer to a small dish, cover and chill until required.
◇ Serve the pâté with pitta bread or a selection of vegetable crudités.

BOTTOM Curried eggs
TOP Aubergine pâté

BACON & MUSHROOM FLAN

~

The availability of ready-made shortcrust pastry enables you to make this flan without having to take the extra time of making your own pastry. However, if you do choose to make it yourself, bake the pastry case blind, and continue as the recipe directs.

═

7 OZ/200 G MADE SHORTCRUST PASTRY

1 TBSP/15 ML OLIVE OIL

8 OZ/225 G RINDLESS SMOKED BACON, CHOPPED

4 OZ/100 G MUSHROOMS, SLICED

2 TSP/10 ML CHOPPED FRESH SAGE

2 EGGS

7 FLOZ/200 ML SINGLE CREAM

PINCH OF GROUND MACE

1½ OZ/40 G GRUYÈRE OR CHEDDAR CHEESE, GRATED

SALT AND PEPPER

═

◇ Roll out the pastry thinly, and use to line an 8 in/20 cm fluted flan tin. Prick the base and chill while preparing the filling. Heat the oven to 240°C/450°F/gas mark 8 and place a baking tray on the centre shelf.
◇ Heat the oil and stir-fry the bacon, over a high heat, until golden. Remove with a slotted spoon and drain.
◇ Add the mushrooms and sage to the pan and stir-fry until just wilted. Drain and cool slightly.
◇ Beat the eggs, cream and seasonings together.
◇ Sprinkle the bacon and mushrooms over the pastry case, pour in the egg mixture and finally top with the grated cheese.
◇ Place in the oven, on the baking tray, and cook for 5 minutes. Lower the temperature to 190°C/375°F/gas mark 5 and cook for a further 20-25 minutes until risen and set. Remove from oven and cool in the tin.
◇ Cover with foil to transport the flan.

COS SALAD WITH BLUE BRIE DRESSING

~

A crisp green salad that is complemented perfectly by this rich, creamy blue cheese dressing.

═

DRESSING

3 OZ/75 G BLUE BRIE

4 TBSP/60 ML OLIVE OIL

3 TBSP/45 ML FROMAGE FRAIS OR YOGURT

4 TSP/20 ML RASPBERRY OR RED WINE VINEGAR

SALT AND PEPPER

SALAD

2 COS LETTUCES

4 OZ/100 G SEEDLESS GREEN GRAPES

2 OZ/50 G YOUNG SPINACH LEAVES OR WATERCRESS

2 YOUNG LEEKS, TRIMMED

1 TBSP/15 ML CHOPPED FRESH CHIVES

2 OZ/50 G PUMPKIN SEEDS, TOASTED

═

◇ Make the dressing: cream the brie, oil and fromage frais or yogurt, in a blender until smooth and stir in the vinegar and seasonings. Pour into a screw-top jar.
◇ Make the salad: wash the lettuce, pat dry and discard the tough outer leaves. Tear into bite-size pieces and place in a large bowl. Halve the grapes, wash and dry the spinach. Finely slice the leeks and add to the lettuce with the chives. Transfer to a container.
◇ Transport the dressing, salad and pumpkin seeds separately and toss together just before serving.

BOTTOM *Bacon and mushroom flan*
TOP *Cos salad with blue brie dressing*

SPINACH TORTILLA

~

A Spanish-style omelette, made with spinach and cottage cheese for a fresh and tasty summer dish. Quick and easy to make, tortillas are great picnic food.

===

1 TBSP/15 ML OLIVE OIL

1 SMALL ONION, CHOPPED

1 MEDIUM POTATO, PEELED AND DICED

½ TSP/1.25 ML GROUND TURMERIC

4 OZ/100 G SPINACH LEAVES, SHREDDED

6 OZ/175 G COTTAGE CHEESE

6 EGGS, LIGHTLY BEATEN

PINCH OF GRATED NUTMEG

SALT AND PEPPER

===

◇ Heat the oil in an 8 in/20 cm non-stick frying pan and sauté the onion, potato and turmeric over a medium heat for 10 minutes, until lightly browned.

◇ Stir in the spinach leaves until they start to wilt.

◇ Beat the cheese and eggs together and pour into the pan. Cook for 15 minutes, until the tortilla is almost set, then place under a hot grill to finish off the top.

◇ Remove from the heat and leave to go cold in the pan.

◇ Turn out on to a plate, cover with foil and keep cool until required.

CARROT & COURGETTE SALAD

~

A refreshingly tangy salad which improves with time as the flavours are allowed to mingle.

===

4 MEDIUM CARROTS, PEELED

4 MEDIUM COURGETTES

1 SMALL RED ONION

1 CLOVE GARLIC

1 TSP/5 ML CHOPPED FRESH TARRAGON

3 TBSP/45 ML EXTRA VIRGIN OLIVE OIL

1 TBSP/15 ML RASPBERRY OR RED WINE VINEGAR

1 OZ/25 G PINENUTS, TOASTED

SALT AND PEPPER

===

◇ Thinly slice the carrots, courgettes, onion and garlic and place in a large bowl. Add the tarragon and plenty of salt and pepper.

◇ Blend the oil and vinegar together and add to the bowl. Toss until the salad is well coated and place in a container.

◇ Transport the nuts in a separate container and sprinkle over the salad just before serving.

LEFT *Spinach tortilla*
RIGHT *Carrot and courgette salad*

CHICKEN LIVER PÂTÉ

~

Serve the pâté with French bread, and try it with a spoonful of redcurrant jelly for a tasty alternative. Set a few herb leaves into the butter if wished: the melted butter will need about 1 hour to set, so if time is short, leave this part out.

8 OZ/225 G CHICKEN LIVERS

5 OZ/150 G UNSALTED BUTTER

1 CLOVE GARLIC, CRUSHED

1 TSP/5 ML CHOPPED FRESH THYME

2 TBSP/30 ML PORT OR BRANDY

TO GARNISH

A FEW PRETTY HERB LEAVES

TO SERVE

FRENCH BREAD

REDCURRANT JELLY (OPTIONAL)

◇ Wash and dry the chicken livers and discard any membrane or discoloured bits.

◇ Heat 1 oz/25 g butter and stir-fry the livers over a high heat until browned on the outside but still pink in the centre. Remove with a slotted spoon and place in a food processor or blender.

◇ Sauté the garlic and thyme for 1 minute, add the port or brandy and scrape the bottom of the pan with a wooden spatula.

◇ Add to the chicken livers, with 3 oz/75 g of remaining butter. Purée until smooth and transfer to a dish.

◇ If you have time, gently melt the remaining 1 oz/25 g butter and pour through a fine sieve, over the pâté. Sit a few herb leaves in the butter and chill until set.

◇ Cover with foil or a tight-fitting lid and transport in a cool box.

◇ Serve the pâté with the bread and a spoonful of redcurrant jelly, if wished.

SAUSAGE, BACON & APRICOT KEBABS

~

Serve these tangy glazed kebabs as a starter.

KEBABS

12 RASHERS STREAKY BACON, RIND REMOVED

12 COCKTAIL SAUSAGES

3 LARGE FIRM APRICOTS, STONED AND QUARTERED

GLAZE

2 TBSP/30 ML APRICOT PRESERVE

2 TSP/10 ML DIJON MUSTARD

1 TSP/5 ML WORCESTERSHIRE SAUCE

1 TSP/5 ML LEMON JUICE

6 BAMBOO SKEWERS

◇ Roll up the bacon into rolls and thread onto the skewers, alternating them with the sausages and apricot quarters.

◇ Mix all the glaze ingredients together and brush over the kebabs.

◇ Place under a preheated grill and cook for 8-10 minutes on each side, brushing frequently with the glaze, until crisp and golden.

◇ Leave to go cold and wrap in foil.

FRONT *Chicken liver pâté*
BACK *Sausage, bacon and apricot kebabs*

PASTA SALAD WITH TUNA SAUCE

~

The pasta is mixed with this tangy dressing while still hot, so it will absorb more flavour as it cools.

═══

12 OZ/350 G TRI-COLOUR PASTA

DRESSING

¼ PINT/150 ML EXTRA VIRGIN OLIVE OIL

2 TBSP/30 ML WHITE WINE VINEGAR

2 TBSP/30 ML TOMATO KETCHUP

1 TSP/5 ML PAPRIKA

¼ TSP/1.25 ML CAYENNE PEPPER

SALAD

1 × 7 OZ/200 G CAN TUNA, DRAINED

1 BUNCH SPRING ONIONS

2 TBSP/30 ML CHOPPED FRESH DILL

═══

◇ Cook the pasta in boiling salted water for 10-12 minutes, until 'al dente' (just done). Drain and place in a large bowl.

◇ Blend the dressing ingredients together until combined and toss with the pasta. Leave to go cold.

◇ Stir in the tuna, onions and dill and place in a container ready to transport.

WATERCRESS & SALMON ROLLS

~

Watercress, canned salmon and ready-made mayonnaise combine to make a tasty filling for fresh bread rolls.

═══

1 BUNCH WATERCRESS

1 TBSP/15 ML CHOPPED FRESH TARRAGON

¼ PINT/150 ML READY-MADE MAYONNAISE

GRATED RIND AND JUICE OF 1 LEMON

2 × 7 OZ/200 G CANS PINK SALMON, DRAINED

PINCH OF GRATED NUTMEG

SALT AND PEPPER

TO SERVE

6 LARGE BREAD ROLLS

WATERCRESS (OPTIONAL)

═══

◇ Wash and dry the watercress, discarding any large stalks. Chop finely and blend with the tarragon, mayonnaise, lemon rind and juice.

◇ Flake the salmon and stir into the mayonnaise with nutmeg, salt and pepper.

◇ Cut the rolls in half and fill with the salmon mixture and extra fresh watercress, if wished. Wrap in waxed paper or foil to transport to the picnic.

BACK *Pasta salad with tuna sauce*
FRONT *Watercress and salmon rolls*

SALADE NIÇOISE

~

This is one of many variations of a classic salad niçoise. I particularly like the addition of canned artichoke hearts, but 3 chopped hard-boiled eggs can be substituted instead.

═══

SALAD

2 × 2 OZ/50 G CANS ANCHOVIES, DRAINED

A LITTLE MILK

4 OZ/100 G FRENCH BEANS, TRIMMED

1 × 14 OZ/400 G CAN ARTICHOKE HEARTS, DRAINED

3 OZ/75 G PITTED BLACK OLIVES

1 TBSP/15 ML CHOPPED FRESH CHIVES

1 TBSP/15 ML CHOPPED FRESH BASIL

6 LARGE TOMATOES, QUARTERED

DRESSING

4 TBSP/60 ML VIRGIN OLIVE OIL

1 TBSP/15 ML BALSAMIC OR RED WINE VINEGAR

2 TSP/10 ML WHOLE GRAIN MUSTARD

PINCH OF SUGAR

SALT AND PEPPER

TO GARNISH

BASIL LEAVES

═══

◇ Soak the drained anchovies in a little milk for 10 minutes, drain, wash under cold water and pat dry.
◇ Blanch the beans in boiling salted water for 1-2 minutes until just tender. Drain, refresh under cold water and pat dry.
◇ Quarter the artichoke hearts or peel and chop the eggs (if using) and place in a large bowl. Add the anchovies, beans, olives, herbs and tomatoes and mix well.
◇ Blend all the dressing ingredients together and pour over the salad. Cover and set aside until required.
◇ Stir the salad and dressing well, garnish with basil leaves and serve with crisp fresh bread.

LEEKS À LA GRECQUE

~

My variation of the classic chilled and marinated vegetable dish. Use tender young leeks for the best results, as they are sweet and need little cooking to become tender.

═══

12 SMALL YOUNG LEEKS, TRIMMED

MARINADE

½ PINT/300 ML DRY WHITE WINE

¼ PINT/150 ML VEGETABLE STOCK

1 TBSP/15 ML WHITE WINE VINEGAR

2 SPRIGS THYME

1 TSP/5 ML FENNEL SEEDS, BRUISED

1 TSP/5 ML CORIANDER SEEDS, BRUISED

½ TSP/2.5 ML WHITE PEPPERCORNS

4 LARGE TOMATOES, PEELED, DE-SEEDED AND CHOPPED

PINCH OF SUGAR

SALT AND PEPPER

TO SERVE

2 OZ/50 G PITTED BLACK OLIVES, CHOPPED

═══

◇ Wash the leeks well and pat dry.
◇ Place in a large shallow pan and add the wine, stock, vinegar, herb and spices. Bring to the boil, cover and simmer gently for 8-10 minutes, until the leeks are just tender. Test them with the point of a sharp knife.
◇ Remove the leeks with a slotted spoon and transfer to a shallow dish to cool.
◇ Add the remaining marinade ingredients to the pan and boil for 5 minutes. Cool slightly and pour over the leeks. Set aside to go cold.
◇ Cover and chill until required and serve topped with chopped black olives.

BOTTOM *Salade Niçoise*
TOP *Leeks à la Grecque*

SICILIAN POTATO SALAD

~

*The ingredients in this tasty potato salad are typical of
many classic Sicilian dishes.*

1 × 2 OZ/50 G CAN ANCHOVIES IN OIL,
DRAINED

A LITTLE MILK

2 LB/900 G NEW POTATOES, SCRUBBED

1 TBSP/15 ML CAPERS, CHOPPED

1 TBSP/15 ML CHOPPED FRESH PARSLEY

1 TSP/5 ML GRATED LEMON RIND

1 TBSP/15 ML LEMON JUICE

1 SMALL CLOVE GARLIC, CRUSHED

3 TBSP/45 ML OLIVE OIL

PEPPER

◇ Place the anchovies in a shallow dish, cover with milk
and leave to soak for 10 minutes. Drain the anchovies,
wash under cold water and pat dry.
◇ Cut the potatoes into bite-size chunks and cook in boil-
ing salted water for 10-12 minutes, until just cooked.
◇ Meanwhile, chop the anchovies and mash with all the
remaining ingredients except the oil. Stir in the oil.
◇ Drain the cooked potatoes and place in a large bowl.
Immediately add the anchovy mixture and mix well.
Leave to go cold.
◇ Transfer to a dish or plastic container, cover and keep
cool until ready to serve.

THREE BEAN SALAD

~

*A combination of fresh and canned beans, fruit and
olives is tossed in a mustard dressing.*

SALAD

6 OZ/175 G FRENCH BEANS, TRIMMED

6 OZ/175 G CANNED BORLOTTI BEANS,
DRAINED

6 OZ/175 G CANNED HARICOT BEANS, DRAINED

6 OZ/175 G CANNED CHICKPEAS, DRAINED

1 RED PEPPER, DE-SEEDED AND SLICED

3 OZ/75 G RAISINS

2 OZ/50 G PITTED GREEN OLIVES, CHOPPED

2 TBSP/30 ML SHREDDED FRESH BASIL LEAVES

DRESSING

4 TBSP/60 ML EXTRA VIRGIN OLIVE OIL

1 TBSP/15 ML RED WINE VINEGAR

2 TSP/10 ML DIJON MUSTARD

1 SMALL CLOVE GARLIC, CRUSHED

½ TSP/2.5 ML GROUND CUMIN

SALT AND PEPPER

◇ Blanch the French beans in boiling water for 1-2
minutes, until just tender. Drain, refresh under cold
water, and pat dry. Place in a large bowl and stir in the remaining salad ingredients.
◇ Blend the dressing ingredients together and pour over
the salad, toss well and transfer to a plastic container.
◇ Keep cool until ready to serve.

BACK *Sicilian potato salad*
FRONT *Three bean salad*

STRAWBERRY CHEESE
WITH SHORTBREAD

~

A sweet/savoury cheese which is simply strawberries and cream cheese, served with melt-in-the mouth shortbread biscuits.

══

SHORTBREAD

6 OZ/175 G PLAIN FLOUR

4 OZ/100 G UNSALTED BUTTER, DICED

2 OZ/50 G SUGAR

½ TSP/2.5 ML GROUND CINNAMON

CHEESE

6 OZ/175 G STRAWBERRIES, HULLED

7 OZ/200 G CREAM CHEESE

PEPPER

══

◇ Make the shortbread: sift the flour into a bowl and rub in the butter until the mixture resembles fine bread-crumbs. Stir in the sugar and spice and work the mixture together to form a firm paste.

◇ Divide in half and roll each piece out to an 8 in/20 cm round. Cut each round into 6 triangles and place on a large greased baking tray.

◇ Bake in a preheated oven at 190°C/375°F/gas mark 5 for 15 minutes, until golden. Remove from the oven and cool on a wire rack.

◇ Meanwhile, prepare the cheese: finely chop the strawberries and drain on kitchen paper. Carefully mix with the cheese and pepper and transfer to a small dish with a tight fitting lid. Chill until required.

◇ Transport the dish in a cool box and serve with the shortbread biscuits.

SUMMER BERRY FOOL

~

Fruit fools are wonderfully fresh and fragrant, with a high proportion of fruit purée to cream. The mixture for this fool should be just thick, almost holding its shape. Use your favourite summer berry for this recipe – I prefer loganberries, but raspberries, blackberries or strawberries would work equally well.

══

1½ LB/675 G LOGANBERRIES OR OTHER BERRIES

3-4 OZ/75-100 G ICING SUGAR

3 TBSP/45 ML PORT

8 FL.OZ/225 ML DOUBLE CREAM

TO SERVE

SWEET BISCUITS (BRANDY SNAPS, TUILES OR SHORTBREAD)

══

◇ Purée the fruit in a food processor or blender and pass through a fine sieve to remove the pips. Transfer to a mixing bowl.

◇ Sift in the sugar, beat well until combined and stir in the port.

◇ Lightly whip the cream and gradually beat in the fruit mixture until just thick.

◇ Transfer to a plastic container with a tight-fitting lid and chill until required.

◇ Transport the fool in its container, or in a thermos flask, in a cool box and serve in individual glasses or bowls with the biscuits of your choice.

TOP LEFT *Strawberry cheese with shortbread*
BOTTOM RIGHT *Summer berry fool*

RICOTTA, NUT &
HONEY CHEESE

~

This recipe is based on a classic Spanish sweet, made here with ricotta cheese. It is delightful.

═══

12 OZ/350 G RICOTTA OR CURD CHEESE

2 OZ/50 G PINENUTS, TOASTED

4 TSP/20 ML CLEAR HONEY

½ TSP/2.5 ML GROUND CINNAMON

¼ TSP/1.25 ML FRESHLY GRATED NUTMEG

TO SERVE

SELECTION OF FRESH FRUIT (FIGS, DATES,
NECTARINES, PEARS, APPLES, STRAWBERRIES)

═══

◇ Place the cheese in a bowl. Chop the pinenuts and stir into the ricotta with the remaining ingredients.
◇ Line a sieve with a large piece of muslin and spoon in the cheese mixture. Pull over the ends of the muslin and sit the sieve over a bowl. Place a heavy weight on top and leave to drain for 30 minutes or until required.
◇ Remove the weight and transfer the mixture, in the muslin, to a plastic container.
◇ Transport in a cool box and serve straight from the muslin, with a selection of your favourite fruits.

REFRIGERATOR CAKE

~

This is a no-cook chocolate and gingernut cake which needs to be chilled for about 1 hour in order to firm up, before transporting to the picnic. Make it the first dish you prepare and your forward planning will be well rewarded.

═══

8 OZ/225 G GINGERNUTS, ROUGHLY CRUSHED

4 OZ/100 G DRIED FIGS, FINELY CHOPPED

3 TBSP/45 ML COCOA POWDER

1 TBSP/15 ML CHOPPED STEM GINGER

3 OZ/75 G UNSALTED BUTTER

3 OZ/75 G PLAIN CHOCOLATE

2 TBSP/30 ML STEM GINGER SYRUP

═══

◇ Lightly oil and base line a 7 in/18 cm loose-bottom cake tin and set your refrigerator to its coldest setting.
◇ Combine the gingernuts, figs, 2 tbsp/30 ml cocoa powder and stem ginger in a bowl.
◇ Melt the butter, chocolate and ginger syrup together in a small pan and pour into the bowl. Stir well until the biscuits are coated and spoon into the prepared tin. Press into the sides and smooth the surface.
◇ Chill for 1 hour until firm. Sift over the final 1 tbsp/15 ml cocoa powder, cover the tin with foil and transport in a cool box. Serve cut into wedges.

CENTRE *Ricotta, nut and honey cheese*
RIGHT *Refrigerator cake*

SPARKLING FRUIT CUP

~

The mixed fruit is macerated in the port and brandy and served with chilled sparkling wine.

═══

2 FLOZ/50 ML PORT

2 FLOZ/50 ML BRANDY

2 NECTARINES OR PEACHES, STONED AND SLICED

12 STRAWBERRIES, HULLED AND HALVED

12 RASPBERRIES

1 × 75 CL BOTTLE CHILLED SPARKLING WINE

═══

◇ Combine the port, brandy and fruit together and place in a plastic container, with a tight-fitting lid.
◇ Chill until required and top up with the chilled wine just before serving.

ORCHARD BLOOM

~

A purée of pears and cinnamon, topped up with sparkling apple juice, makes a wonderful thirst-quenching summer drink.

═══

PURÉE

3 LARGE RIPE PEARS, PEELED, CORED AND CHOPPED

1 TSP/5 ML GROUND CINNAMON

1 TSP/5 ML LEMON JUICE

1 TSP/5 ML SUGAR

TO SERVE

1 × 75 CL BOTTLE CHILLED SPARKLING APPLE JUICE

CRUSHED ICE

═══

◇ Place the pears, cinnamon, lemon juice and sugar in a small pan and simmer, covered, over a very low heat for 12-15 minutes, until the pears are soft.
◇ Cool slightly and purée until smooth. Leave to go cold and spoon into a screw-top jar. Chill until required.
◇ Divide the purée between 6 medium tumblers and pour in the apple juice. Add the crushed ice and serve.

PINK PERIL

~

Aptly named for its vibrant colour and deceptive kick! The measures in this recipe are given for a single serving. Use ruby grapefruit if available.

═══

CHILLED VODKA

CRUSHED ICE

2 FLOZ/50 ML FRESHLY SQUEEZED GRAPEFRUIT JUICE

2 FLOZ/50 ML CRANBERRY JUICE

TO DECORATE

MARASCHINO CHERRIES

═══

◇ Pour a measure of vodka into a small cocktail glass and add a little crushed ice.
◇ Top up with the grapefruit and cranberry juices and decorate the glass with a maraschino cherry.
◇ Serve at once.

CENTRE *Sparkling fruit cup*
LEFT *Orchard bloom*
RIGHT *Pink peril*

FOOD WITH FIRE

The mouth-watering aroma and tantalizing flavour absorbed by the food from the charcoal during cooking make barbecues increasingly popular throughout the world. With a few exceptions, the recipes in this chapter are for food that can be cooked on a barbecue or over hot coals. (There are also a couple of recipes for appetizers, which you can pass around while the barbecue is being prepared, and some desserts, which you can make in advance to finish off the meal.)
There is a range of different types of barbecue available, from small portable ones to the gas or electric type, or even the disposable foil-tray varieties. But you can have much fun constructing one at home with a few bricks, a metal tray for the coals and a grid for the food.
Camp fires are an attractive alternative to the barbecue, and need little else than some dry wood, matches and a little enthusiasm and patience! You can use lumpwood charcoal (but it tends to burn rather quickly) or superior charcoal briquettes (made from dense hardwood, with a low-resin content), which provide a more intense and uniform heat. Good-quality solid firelighters, specially designed for barbecues, will help you get the fire started.
The coals will be ready for cooking over when the flames have died away and you are left with glowing, slightly ashen coals. Place the food on a lightly oiled grid, an inch or two above the coals (but do not do this too soon or it will become tainted by the flames).
Safety is very much a case of common sense: site the barbecue away from the house, trees, or a confined space; don't use petrol, lighter fuels, or similar flammable liquids to light the coals; don't leave matches next to the barbecue; use long-handled tongs and other tools to avoid burns; and if using a transportable barbecue, allow it to cool completely before packing it away.

CONTENTS

LENTIL & CASHEW NUT SOUP

~

A creamy heart-warming soup, ideal for an autumn evening barbecue.

═══

2 TBSP/30 ML OLIVE OIL

1 LARGE ONION, CHOPPED

1 CLOVE GARLIC, CRUSHED

8 OZ/225 G CARROTS, CHOPPED

2 TSP/10 ML GROUND CORIANDER

1 TSP/5 ML GROUND CUMIN

½ TSP/2.5 ML GROUND TURMERIC

½ TSP/2.5 ML GROUND CINNAMON

4 OZ/100 G RED LENTILS, WASHED

1¾ PINT/1 L CHICKEN OR VEGETABLE STOCK

1 BAYLEAF

4 OZ/100 G CASHEW NUTS, TOASTED

JUICE OF 1 LEMON

SALT AND PEPPER

═══

◇ Heat the oil in a large saucepan and fry the onion and garlic for 5 minutes, until lightly browned. Add the carrots and spices and stir-fry for 2-3 minutes, until the vegetables are well coated.

◇ Add the lentils, stock and bayleaf, bring to the boil, cover and simmer gently for 20 minutes, until the lentils and carrots are soft.

◇ Remove the bayleaf and purée the soup in a food processor or blender until smooth and return to the pan.

◇ Grind the nuts and lemon juice to a rough paste in a blender or food processor, stir into the soup, heat through and season to taste. Alternatively, transport the nuts in a separate container and add to the soup before serving.

◇ Transfer the soup to a thermos flask to keep hot.

MOROCCAN SPICED GARLIC BREAD

~

Add a little spice to your life with this Moroccan version of garlic bread. This recipe will serve 6 or 12 people depending on how hungry they are.

═══

2 SMALL FRENCH STICKS

6 OZ/175 G BUTTER, SOFTENED

2 CLOVES GARLIC, CRUSHED

1 TBSP/15 ML TOMATO PURÉE

1 TBSP/15 ML CHOPPED FRESH CORIANDER

1 TBSP/15 ML CHOPPED FRESH PARSLEY

½ TSP/2.5 ML GROUND CUMIN

½ TSP/2.5 ML GROUND PAPRIKA

PINCH OF CAYENNE PEPPER

SALT

═══

◇ Cut the bread into ½ in/1 cm slices, without cutting right the way through to the bottom.

◇ Cream all the remaining ingredients together and spread a little spiced butter between each bread slice. Spread any remaining butter all over the bread.

◇ Wrap the bread sticks in foil and turn the edges over to seal.

◇ Bake the bread in a preheated oven at 200°C/400°F/ gas mark 6 for 10 minutes, open the foil and bake for a further 5 minutes. Alternatively, place the foil parcels over the coolest part of a hot barbecue and cook for 5 minutes, turn over and cook for a further 5 minutes.

◇ Serve piping hot.

FRONT *Lentil and cashew nut soup*
BACK *Moroccan spiced garlic bread*

PRAWN & MONKFISH KEBABS WITH COCONUT SALSA

~

The tantalizing aroma of these kebabs cooking on the barbecue is certain to get your taste buds going. They are quick to cook and, served with this unusual coconut salsa, are quite delicious.

═══

SALSA

7 FLOZ/200 ML OLIVE OIL

2 TSP/10 ML SESAME OIL

8 SPRING ONIONS, TRIMMED AND FINELY CHOPPED

2 TBSP/30 ML CHOPPED FRESH CORIANDER

RIND AND JUICE OF 2 LIMES

1-2 DRIED RED CHILLIES, CRUSHED

2 OZ/50 G DESICCATED COCONUT

KEBABS

18 RAW MEDITERRANEAN PRAWNS

1 LB/450 G MONKFISH FILLETS

4 LIMES, SLICED

6 METAL SKEWERS

SESAME OIL FOR BASTING

═══

◇ Make the salsa: heat both oils together in a small pan and sauté the onion and coriander for 2 minutes. Remove from the heat and stir in the remaining ingredients. Transfer to a small dish and leave to cool.
◇ Wash and dry the prawns and, if preferred, remove the heads and shells. Cut the monkfish into 1 in/2.5 cm pieces.
◇ Thread the prawns, monkfish and lime slices alternately onto the metal skewers, brush all over with sesame oil and place on the barbecue. Cook the kebabs for 6-8 minutes turning and basting with oil, from time to time, until the prawns and monkfish are lightly charred and cooked through.
◇ Serve at once with the coconut salsa.

PERSIAN CHICKEN KEBABS

~

A unique blend of nuts, spices and yogurt make these chicken kebabs an unusual and exotic dish. Use 2 skewers to make each kebab, as the chicken pieces are quite large.

═══

12 CHICKEN THIGHS

MARINADE

7 FLOZ/200 ML GREEK YOGURT

1 SMALL ONION, MINCED

2 LARGE CLOVES GARLIC, CRUSHED

2 OZ/50 G CASHEW NUTS, TOASTED AND GROUND

JUICE OF 1 LEMON

1 TSP/5 ML GROUND CUMIN

1 TSP/5 ML GROUND MIXED SPICE

PINCH OF CAYENNE PEPPER

SALT AND PEPPER

TO SERVE

LEMON WEDGES

12 BAMBOO SKEWERS

═══

◇ Skin the chicken and cut out the bone. Cut each one in half and place in a large bowl.
◇ Blend the marinade ingredients together until combined and pour into the bowl. Stir well until the chicken pieces are well coated. Cover and marinate for at least 4 hours or overnight.
◇ Soak the skewers in cold water for 30 minutes. Pat dry and thread the chicken pieces onto each pair of skewers to make 6 large kebabs.
◇ Cook over a hot barbecue for 7-8 minutes on each side, until the chicken is lightly charred all over.
◇ Serve the kebabs hot with lemon wedges.

BACK *Prawn and monkfish kebabs with coconut salsa*
FRONT *Persian chicken kebabs*

RED MULLET
WITH FENNEL

~

This firm-fleshed fish is ideal to barbecue, and has few nasty little bones to contend with. The aroma of the fennel and red mullet barbecuing together is truly mouthwatering.

═══

6 × 6 OZ/175 G RED MULLET, SCALED AND GUTTED

2 SMALL FENNEL BULBS, THICKLY SLICED

MARINADE

½ PINT/300 ML OLIVE OIL

3 FLOZ/75 ML DRY WHITE WINE

1 CLOVE GARLIC, ROUGHLY CHOPPED

1 SMALL RED CHILLI, SEEDED AND SLICED

4 SPRIGS THYME, BRUISED

2 SPRIGS PARSLEY, BRUISED

1 TSP/5 ML CORIANDER SEEDS, ROUGHLY CRUSHED

½ TSP/2.5 ML FENNEL SEEDS

SALT AND PEPPER

═══

◇ Wash the mullet inside and out and dry well. Cut 3 small slashes through the skin of the fish on both sides, and place in a large, shallow dish. Add the fennel slices.
◇ Mix the marinade ingredients together and pour over the fish. Cover and leave to marinate for several hours or overnight, turning the fish and fennel occasionally.
◇ Remove the mullet and fennel from the marinade. Barbecue the fish for 4-5 minutes on each side and the fennel for 2-3 minutes on each side until both are cooked and lightly charred. Baste with the marinade if necessary.
◇ Serve immediately with Tomato and Olive Oil Bruschetta and a crisp green salad.

TOMATO & OLIVE
OIL BRUSCHETTA

~

An Italian-style garlic toast, topped with juicy tomatoes, bruschetta can either be grilled conventionally and served while the barbecue is being prepared, or the bread can be toasted over the hot coals and served as an accompanying dish. Both methods are given, and either way it's delicious.

═══

1 SMALL CIABATTA LOAF (ITALIAN OLIVE OIL BREAD) OR FRENCH STICK

2 CLOVES GARLIC, HALVED

6 LARGE RIPE TOMATOES, THINLY SLICED

6 LARGE BASIL LEAVES, SHREDDED

ABOUT 3 FLOZ/75 ML VIRGIN OLIVE OIL

SALT AND PEPPER

═══

◇ To grill: slice the bread in half lengthways and grill on both sides for 1-2 minutes.
◇ Rub the garlic cloves all over the toast, and top with the tomato slices, basil leaves and salt and pepper.
◇ Drizzle liberally with oil and grill for 3-4 minutes, or until the tomatoes are sizzling.
◇ Cut into fingers and serve piping hot.

◇ To barbecue: marinate the tomatoes, basil, oil and seasonings together for 30 minutes.
◇ Slice the bread in half lengthways and toast both sides over the barbecue until lightly golden. Rub the garlic all over the toast and top with the marinated tomato mixture. Cut into fingers and serve.

BOTTOM *Red mullet with fennel*
TOP *Tomato and olive oil bruschetta*

GLAZED LAMB STEAKS

~

Infused by the flavours of the marinade, these succulent lamb steaks are spread with honey and mustard, which becomes a crisp golden glaze when barbecued.

6 LAMB STEAKS

MARINADE

3 CLOVES GARLIC, HALVED

6 SPRIGS MINT, BRUISED

6 SPRIGS ROSEMARY, BRUISED

¼ PINT/150 ML OLIVE OIL

SALT AND PEPPER

GLAZE

9 TBSP/135 ML WHOLEGRAIN MUSTARD

3 TBSP/45 ML CLEAR HONEY

3 TBSP/45 ML CHOPPED FRESH MINT

◇ Wash and dry the steaks and rub all over with the garlic, salt and pepper. Lay half the mint and rosemary sprigs in the base of a large shallow dish. Place the lamb on top and cover with the remaining herbs. Pour over the oil, cover and marinate for several hours or overnight.
◇ Remove the steaks from the marinade and pat dry.
◇ Mix the glaze ingredients together and spread all over the lamb steaks.
◇ Cook on the prepared barbecue for 6-8 minutes on each side, until the lamb is glazed and cooked through. The meat should still be slightly pink in the middle.
◇ Serve the lamb steaks hot with Foil-Baked Mushrooms (see page 52) and Char-Grilled Peppers (see page 48).

SOUTHERN CHICKEN WINGS WITH SPICY BARBECUE SAUCE

~

This spicy sauce is an old favourite and is highly recommended by all who have tried it.

SAUCE

½ PINT/300 ML TOMATO KETCHUP

6 TBSP/90 ML CLEAR HONEY

4 TBSP/60 ML WORCESTERSHIRE SAUCE OR 2 TSP/30 ML TABASCO

2 TBSP/30 ML WHITE WINE VINEGAR

2 TSP/10 ML MUSTARD

18 CHICKEN WINGS

◇ Blend the sauce ingredients together until smooth.
◇ Brush the chicken wings with a little sauce and place over a hot barbecue. Cook for 15-20 minutes, turning and basting frequently until the glaze is crisp and golden, and the chicken is tender.
◇ Allow to cool slightly before serving with Baked Sweet Potatoes with Garlic and Thyme (see page 52) and a fresh summer salad.

RIGHT *Glazed lamb steaks*
LEFT *Southern chicken wings with spicy barbecue sauce*

BEEF & VEGETABLE KEBABS WITH HERBY YOGURT SAUCE

~

Cubes of beef and mixed vegetables are marinated, threaded onto skewers, barbecued and served with a herby yogurt sauce.

KEBABS

2 LB/900 G LEAN BEEF

12 BABY ONIONS

24 BUTTON MUSHROOMS

2 RED PEPPERS

2 YELLOW PEPPERS

4 LARGE COURGETTES

MARINADE

¼ PINT/150 ML OLIVE OIL

1 TBSP/15 ML LEMON JUICE

1 TBSP/15 ML CORIANDER SEEDS, CRUSHED

2 TSP/10 ML CUMIN SEEDS, CRUSHED

2 SPRIGS THYME, BRUISED

2 SPRIGS SAGE, BRUISED

1 TSP/5 ML FRESH GREEN PEPPERCORNS, CRUSHED

PINCH OF FRESHLY GRATED NUTMEG

SAUCE

½ PINT/300 ML NATURAL YOGURT

1 TBSP/15 ML LEMON JUICE

1 TBSP/15 ML CHOPPED FRESH MINT

1 TBSP/15 ML CHOPPED FRESH DILL

1 TSP/5 ML GROUND CUMIN

PINCH OF CAYENNE PEPPER

SALT AND PEPPER

24 BAYLEAVES

12 METAL SKEWERS

◇ Cut the beef into cubes. Prepare the vegetables: peel and halve the onions, wash and dry the mushrooms, deseed the peppers and cut each one into 12 pieces. Wash and dry the courgettes and cut into 6×1 in/2.5 cm slices.

◇ Place the beef and vegetables in a large bowl.

◇ Prepare the marinade: blend the oil and lemon juice together, pour into the bowl and add the remaining marinade ingredients. Toss well together, cover and leave to marinate for several hours or overnight.

◇ Prepare the sauce: blend all the ingredients together in a small bowl and set aside.

◇ 30 minutes before assembling the kebabs, soak the bayleaves in cold water. Drain and pat dry.

◇ Thread the beef, vegetables and bayleaves alternately on to the metal skewers and cook over a hot barbecue for 15 minutes. Turn the kebabs and baste frequently with any marinade or extra olive oil. The beef and vegetables should be browned and tender.

◇ Serve 2 kebabs per person with a generous spoonful of the herby yogurt sauce.

Beef and vegetable kebabs with herby yogurt sauce

CHINESE SPICED RIBLETS

~

Riblets are ribs that have been cut in half to make them easier to handle. Boiling the riblets in water and vinegar tenderizes the meat which is then cooked quickly over a hot barbecue, to become succulent and crispy.

═

2 LB/900 G PORK SPARE RIBLETS

3 TBSP/45 ML WINE VINEGAR

3 TBSP/45 ML CLEAR HONEY

3 TBSP/45 ML YELLOW BEAN PASTE

1 TBSP/15 ML SOY SAUCE

1 TBSP/15 ML DRY SHERRY

2 TSP/10 ML SHERRY VINEGAR

1 IN/2.5 CM FRESH ROOT GINGER, PEELED

½ TSP/2.5 ML CHINESE FIVE SPICE POWDER

PINCH OF CAYENNE PEPPER

═

◇ Place the riblets in a large saucepan, add the wine vinegar and enough water to cover. Bring to the boil and simmer gently for 20 minutes, skimming the surface from time to time. Drain and allow to cool.
◇ Blend the honey, yellow bean paste, soy sauce, sherry and sherry vinegar together. Crush the ginger in a garlic crush to extract the juice and add to the honey mixture with the spices. Pour over the riblets and leave to marinate for several hours, turning frequently.
◇ Barbecue the spiced riblets, for 5 minutes on each side, basting them as they cook.
◇ Serve hot.

BACON & BANANA KEBABS

~

Try this combination of sweet and savoury and you will be pleasantly surprised at how well they marry together.

═

36 LARGE SAGE LEAVES

9 RASHERS STREAKY BACON

3 LARGE BANANAS

12 BAMBOO SKEWERS

═

◇ Soak the skewers in water for 30 minutes. Soak the sage leaves for 10 minutes then pat dry.
◇ De-rind the bacon and cut in half crossways. Stretch each half to double its length, by running the blunt edge of a knife along it.
◇ Peel and cut each banana into 4 large chunks.
◇ Wrap the stretched bacon around the bananas and thread onto the skewers with a sage leaf dividing each banana chunk. Place over a hot barbecue and cook for 3-4 minutes on each side, until the bacon is crisp and golden.
◇ Serve at once as a starter.

BACK *Chinese spiced riblets*
FRONT *Bacon and banana kebabs*

CHAR-GRILLED PEPPERS

~

The smoky flavour the barbecue gives these peppers is exquisite.

══

6 LARGE PEPPERS, RED, YELLOW AND ORANGE

DRESSING

4 TBSP/60 ML HAZELNUT OR OLIVE OIL

2 TSP/10 ML BALSAMIC VINEGAR

1 LARGE CLOVE GARLIC, CHOPPED

2 TBSP/30 ML CHOPPED FRESH BASIL

SALT AND PEPPER

══

◇ Place the peppers over a hot barbecue and cook, turning frequently until the skins blister and become charred.
◇ Put the peppers in a plastic bag and leave to cool and soften for 30 minutes. Peel and discard the skins and seeds, over a bowl to reserve the juices. Cut the flesh into thick slices.
◇ Pour the pepper juices into a bowl and blend in all the dressing ingredients, except the basil. Pour the dressing over the peppers and sprinkle over the basil.
◇ Serve warm or cold.

SESAME COURGETTES

~

A delicious way of cooking courgettes. They are brushed liberally with sesame oil, barbecued and served with a sesame and rosemary dressing.

══

6 LARGE COURGETTES

SESAME OIL TO BRUSH

DRESSING

6 TBSP/90 ML SESAME OIL

2 TBSP/30 ML LEMON JUICE

1 TBSP/15 ML CHOPPED FRESH ROSEMARY

PINCH OF SUGAR

SALT AND PEPPER

══

◇ Cut each courgette into 4 thick slices and brush with sesame oil. Cook over a hot barbecue for 2-3 minutes on each side, until browned.
◇ Place in a shallow dish, blend the dressing ingredients together and pour over the courgettes.
◇ Serve hot, warm or cold.

TOP *Char-grilled peppers*
BOTTOM *Sesame courgettes*

TUNA FISH SATÉ

~

Fresh tuna is the perfect fish for this Thai-style saté, as its rich flavour and meaty texture are not overpowered by the soy marinade and peanut sauce.

2 LB/900 G FRESH TUNA STEAKS

MARINADE

3 TBSP/45 ML LIGHT SOY SAUCE

2 TBSP/30 ML WATER

1 TBSP/15 ML SESAME OIL

1 TBSP/15 ML CLEAR HONEY

1 TBSP/15 ML DRY SHERRY

JUICE OF 1 LIME

1 CLOVE GARLIC, CRUSHED

1 IN/2.5 CM PIECE ROOT GINGER, GRATED

SAUCE

4 TBSP/60 ML RAW PEANUTS, GROUND

JUICE OF 1 LIME

2 TBSP/30 ML WATER

½ OZ/15 G CREAMED COCONUT

¼ TSP/1.25 ML CAYENNE PEPPER

PINCH OF SUGAR

◇ Wash and dry the tuna and cut into ½ in/1 cm cubes.
◇ Blend the marinade ingredients together and pour over the fish in a large shallow dish. Cover and leave to marinate for 1-2 hours, turning the fish over occasionally.
◇ Drain and reserve the marinade and thread 6 cubes of tuna onto each skewer. Cover and keep cool.
◇ Make the sauce: put 6 tbsp/90 ml of reserved marinade into a small pan and bring to the boil. Stir in the remaining sauce ingredients and simmer over a low heat, until the coconut melts and the sauce thickens slightly. Transfer to a small bowl and leave to cool.
◇ Cook the tuna saté over a hot barbecue for 5-6 minutes, turning frequently and basting with the rest of the marinade, until cooked. Serve with peanut sauce.

PAN-FRIED FISH STEAKS

~

I love the Spanish way of cooking fish on a 'plancha' or griddle, over hot coals, and firm-fleshed fish are particularly good cooked this way.

6×6 OZ/175 G SWORDFISH, HALIBUT OR
SALMON STEAKS

MARINADE

¼ PINT/150 ML OLIVE OIL

12 BAYLEAVES, BRUISED

3 CARDAMOM PODS, BRUISED

1 TBSP/15 ML CHOPPED FRESH PARSLEY

1 TBSP/15 ML GROUND PAPRIKA

6 LEMON SLICES

SAUCE

6 TBSP/90 ML OLIVE OIL

JUICE OF 1 LEMON

1 CLOVE GARLIC, CRUSHED

1 TBSP/15 ML CHOPPED FRESH PARSLEY

PINCH OF CAYENNE PEPPER

SALT

◇ Wash and dry the fish and place in a large shallow dish.
◇ Pour in the oil and add the remaining marinade ingredients. Cover and marinate for 2-3 hours, turning the fish over from time to time.
◇ Make the sauce: beat the oil and lemon juice together until thickened and add garlic, parsley, cayenne and salt.
◇ Place the griddle over the barbecue, brush with oil and allow it to get really hot. Fry the fish on both sides for 4-6 minutes, until golden and firm to the touch.
◇ Alternatively, place the fish directly over the heat on the barbecue grid and cook for 4-6 minutes on each side.
◇ Serve the fish with plenty of lemon and garlic sauce poured over, and a fresh green salad.

LEFT *Tuna fish saté*
RIGHT *Pan-fried fish steaks*

BAKED SWEET POTATOES
WITH GARLIC & THYME

~

Cooking these sweet potatoes in a double layer of foil seals in their delicious flavour. Ordinary potatoes can be cooked in the same way, but may need a little extra time to cook.

═══

1½ LB/675 G SWEET POTATOES, PEELED

6 LARGE PIECES FOIL, FOLDED IN HALF

12 UNPEELED CLOVES GARLIC

12 SPRIGS THYME

3 OZ/75 G BUTTER, DICED

SALT AND PEPPER

═══

◇ Cut the potatoes into small chunks and divide between the 6 double layers of foil.
◇ To each pile of potatoes add 2 cloves garlic, 2 sprigs thyme, a few bits of butter and plenty salt and pepper.
◇ Pull the edges of the foil up and turn over to completely seal the fillings.
◇ Place the parcels over a hot barbecue and cook for 20-25 minutes, until the potatoes are tender. Serve straight from the foil.

FOIL-BAKED
MUSHROOMS

~

All the flavour and juices from the mushrooms stay sealed within the foil parcels, making a tasty starter or an accompaniment to other barbecued food.

═══

18 SMALL FLAT-CAP MUSHROOMS

6 LARGE PIECES FOIL, FOLDED IN HALF

3 OZ/75 G BUTTER, SOFTENED

1 CLOVE GARLIC, CRUSHED

1 TBSP/15 ML CHOPPED FRESH SAGE

GRATED RIND OF 1 LEMON

SALT AND PEPPER

═══

◇ Place 3 mushrooms in the centre of each double layer of foil.
◇ Cream together the butter, garlic, sage, lemon rind and salt and pepper and spread a spoonful over each mushroom. Pull the edges of the foil up and turn over to seal the fillings.
◇ Place over a hot barbecue for 6-8 minutes until the mushrooms are tender and juicy.
◇ Serve straight from the foil.

BOTTOM *Baked sweet potatoes with garlic and thyme*
TOP *Foil-baked mushrooms*

FRUIT KEBABS WITH HONEY GLAZE

~

Finish your meal with these succulent, lightly caramelized fruit kebabs.

═══

KEBABS

1 SMALL MANGO, PEELED AND STONED

½ SMALL PINEAPPLE (CUT LENGTHWAYS), PEELED

2 SMALL DESSERT APPLES

2 LARGE BANANAS, PEELED

24 KUMQUATS

GLAZE

¼ PINT/150 ML CLEAR HONEY

SHREDDED RIND AND JUICE OF 1 ORANGE

¼ TSP/1.25 ML GROUND CLOVES

12 BAMBOO SKEWERS

═══

◇ Cut the mango flesh into 12 chunks. Halve the pine-apple, remove the centre core, and cut each quarter into 6 slices. Cut the apples into 12 wedges, cut the bananas into 12 thick slices and wash and dry the kumquats.

◇ Thread 2 kumquats and 1 piece each of the other prepared fruits onto each skewer. Place in large shallow dish.

◇ Blend the glaze ingredients together and pour over the kebabs. Cover and marinate for 30 minutes, turning once.

◇ Cook over a hot barbecue for 6-8 minutes, turning and basting frequently with the glaze, until the fruit is browned and sizzling.

◇ Serve hot.

FOILED RUM BANANAS

~

Serve these foil-wrapped bananas straight from the barbecue with a spoonful of whipped cream or yogurt.

═══

6 MEDIUM BANANAS, PEELED

6 LARGE PIECES FOIL, FOLDED IN HALF

2 TBSP/30 ML CHOPPED STEM GINGER

2 TBSP/30 ML STEM GINGER SYRUP

4 TBSP/60 ML DARK RUM

2 TBSP/30 ML ORANGE JUICE

2 OZ/50 G UNSALTED BUTTER

═══

◇ Cut each banana in half lengthways and place on the centre of each double layer of foil.

◇ Pull the edges up leaving a small gap at the top and add 1 tsp/5 ml chopped ginger, 1 tsp/5 ml syrup, 2 tsp/10 ml rum, 1 tsp/5ml orange juice and a little of the butter to each parcel. Turn the edges over to seal well.

◇ Bake over a hot barbecue for 5-6 minutes until the bananas are succulent and tender.

◇ Serve immediately with a little cream or yogurt.

TOP AND LEFT *Fruit kebabs with honey glaze*
BOTTOM RIGHT *Foiled rum bananas*

APRICOT & PISTACHIO TART

~

This fresh apricot tart tastes as good as it looks, with a layer of apricots arranged over a creamy pistachio custard in a crispy pastry case.

═══

PASTRY

6 OZ/175 G PLAIN FLOUR

PINCH OF SALT

4 OZ/100 G UNSALTED BUTTER

2 TBSP/30 ML SUGAR

1 EGG YOLK

PISTACHIO CUSTARD

8 FLOZ/225 ML MILK

3 EGG YOLKS

2 OZ/50 G SUGAR

2 OZ/50 G PLAIN FLOUR

½ OZ/15 G UNSALTED BUTTER

2½ OZ/60 G PISTACHIO NUTS, GROUND

GLAZE

3 TBSP/45 ML APRICOT PRESERVE

1 TSP/5 ML LEMON JUICE

TOPPING

1¼-1½ LB/500-675 G APRICOTS, BLANCHED,
PEELED, HALVED AND STONED

½ OZ/15 G SHELLED PISTACHIO NUTS

═══

◇ Sift the flour and salt into a bowl and rub in the butter. Stir in the sugar and work in the egg yolk and 1 tbsp/15 ml cold water to form a firm paste. Wrap and chill.
◇ Roll out the pastry and line a 9 in/23 cm fluted flan tin. Prick the base and chill for 15 minutes.
◇ Bake blind in a preheated oven at 200°C/400°F/gas mark 6 for 15 minutes. Remove the beans and foil and bake for a further 12-15 minutes until crisp and golden.
◇ Prepare the pistachio custard: heat the milk until just boiling. Whisk the egg yolks and sugar until pale and creamy and beat in the flour. Whisk in the milk and pour through a sieve into a clean pan. Heat gently, stirring, until thickened and cook over a low heat for 2 minutes.

Remove from the heat and beat in the butter. Cool slightly, stir in the ground nuts and cover with cling film.
◇ Make the glaze: heat the preserve, 1 tsp/5 ml water and the lemon juice, boil for 1 minute and leave to cool.
◇ Spread the custard over the pastry case and arrange the apricots over the top, pressing down gently. Place a pistachio nut between each gap and spoon over the glaze.

PEACH & CINNAMON PUFFS

~

Attractive, individual puff pastry squares, filled with cinnamon paste and sliced peaches. Serve warm or cold with whipped cream or fromage frais.

═══

1½ LB/675 G PUFF PASTRY

3 OZ/75 G UNSALTED BUTTER, SOFTENED

2 OZ/50 G GROUND WALNUTS

1½ OZ/40 G SUGAR

1½ TSP/7.5 ML GROUND CINNAMON

3 PEACHES, PEELED, STONED AND THINLY
SLICED

GLAZE

1 EGG BEATEN WITH 1 TBSP/15 ML MILK

A LITTLE SUGAR

═══

◇ Roll out the pastry thinly and cut into 12, 5 in/13 cm squares. Using a 4½ in/12 cm pastry cutter, stamp out the middle from 6 of the 12 squares. Chill for 30 minutes.
◇ Cream remaining dry ingredients together and spread in a circle over the 6 uncut pastry squares.
◇ Arrange peach slices over the cinnamon paste. Wet the edges of the pastry, lay over the cut pastry squares, and press together to seal. Knock up and flute the edges of the pastry with a sharp knife and chill for 15 minutes.
◇ Heat the oven to 220°C/425°F/gas mark 7. Brush the pastry with the egg glaze and sprinkle a little sugar over the peaches. Bake on a hot baking tray for 12-15 minutes.

LEFT *Apricot and pistachio tart*
RIGHT *Peach and cinnamon puffs*

FOOD WITH FIRE

SANGRIA

~

There are many variations of this classic Spanish aperitif. I was served this by a friend in Majorca. Substitute brandy for the Grand Marnier, if preferred.

═══

1×75 CL BOTTLE LIGHT RED WINE

4 FLOZ/125 ML FRESHLY SQUEEZED ORANGE JUICE

4 TBSP/60 ML GRAND MARNIER

1 ORANGE, THINLY SLICED

1 APPLE, CORED AND THINLY SLICED

1 SMALL LEMON, THINLY SLICED

½ PINT/300 ML FIZZY LEMONADE

TO SERVE

ICE CUBES

═══

◇ Pour the wine into a large punch bowl or jug and stir in the orange juice and Grand Marnier.
◇ Add the fruit and pour in the lemonade, stir well and serve with a handful of ice cubes.

BLUSHING STRAWBERRY FIZZ

~

Crushed fresh strawberries and Cointreau are topped up with champagne to make this summer aperitif.

═══

24 STRAWBERRIES, HULLED

4 TBSP/60 ML COINTREAU

1 BOTTLE CHAMPAGNE

═══

◇ Crush the strawberries and blend with the Cointreau. Divide between 6 glasses and top up with the champagne. Serve immediately.

HOMEMADE LEMONADE

~

Make this lemon syrup and keep refrigerated in a screw-top bottle, diluting it with still or sparkling water, as preferred.

═══

6 LARGE LEMONS

6 WHOLE CLOVES

2 PINT/1.2 LITRE BOILING WATER

1 LB/450 G SUGAR

JUICE OF 2 LEMONS

TO SERVE

1 BOTTLE STILL OR SPARKLING MINERAL WATER

LEMON SLICES

LEMON BALM

ICE CUBES

═══

◇ Wash and dry the lemons and cut into thick slices. Place in a large bowl with the cloves and pour in the boiling water. Leave to infuse for 24 hours.
◇ Drain and discard the lemon slices and cloves. Place the infused liquid in a large pan, add the sugar and heat gently until dissolved. Bring to the boil and simmer for 10 minutes until the liquid is thick and syrupy. Remove from the heat and leave to go cold.
◇ Add the fresh lemon juice and pour into a screw-top bottle, then chill until required.
◇ To serve, put 1-2 tbsp/15-30 ml lemon syrup into each glass, top up with mineral water and decorate with lemon slices and lemon balm if wished, and add ice cubes.

BOTTOM CENTRE *Sangria*
TOP *Blushing strawberry fizz*
BOTTOM LEFT AND RIGHT *Homemade lemonade*

MOVEABLE FEASTS

A forthcoming outing or annual event, such as a sports meeting or fête, can provide the ideal opportunity to prepare a more lavish feast. Some of the recipes in this chapter will take a little more time and effort to prepare than those in Picnics to Go, but all are ideal for a special picnic and are easily transportable.

This is the occasion to indulge your fantasies of the great picnics that have been a tradition for centuries. It is easy to conjure up the image of sitting down at an elegantly arranged table, surrounded by exotic and evocative dishes, and the recipes here have been created to make this a practical possibility. For a particularly special occasion why not splash out and buy a picnic hamper? They are long lasting and a good investment for future parties. If you have the space, why not include a folding table and chairs, linen and silverware and, for an evening picnic, take along a lantern or several candles, which are not only practical, but can also look very appealing.

A whole feast can be composed with the following recipes and you will be guaranteed a picnic fit for a king.

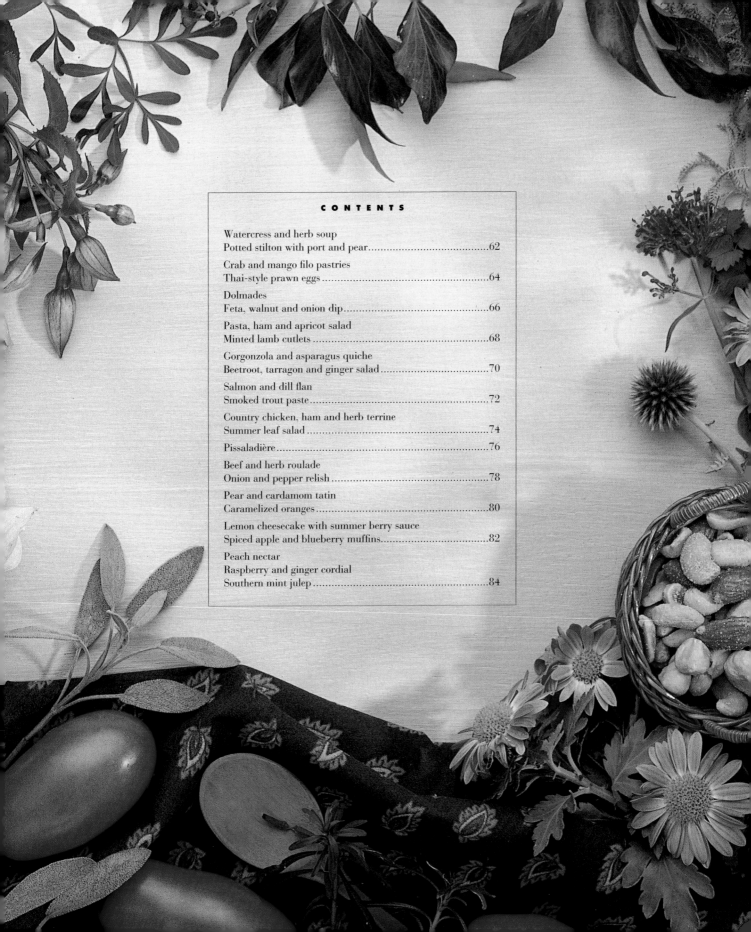

CONTENTS

WATERCRESS & HERB SOUP

~

A fresh, light summer soup. Add the ground almonds if you want a slightly more substantial soup, or if the weather demands a more warming one!

═══

1 OZ/25 G BUTTER

1 LARGE ONION, CHOPPED

1 CLOVE GARLIC, CRUSHED

8 OZ/225 G WATERCRESS

4 TBSP/60 ML CHOPPED FRESH HERBS (BASIL, CHERVIL, CHIVES, MINT, THYME)

1¼ PINT/750 ML VEGETABLE STOCK

¼ PINT/150 ML MILK

2 OZ/50 G ALMONDS, TOASTED AND GROUND (OPTIONAL)

SALT AND PEPPER

═══

◇ Heat the butter and sauté the onion and garlic for 5 minutes. Stir in the watercress and herbs and pour in the stock and milk.

◇ Bring to the boil, cover and simmer gently for 15 minutes.

◇ Purée the soup in a food processor or blender, until fairly smooth. Heat through, add the almonds if wished, season to taste and pour into a thermos flask.

POTTED STILTON WITH PORT & PEAR

~

Press the stilton mixture into a pretty dish with a lid, and serve with plenty of fresh celery. This will keep for several days in the refrigerator.

═══

2 OZ/50 G LOW-FAT CREAM CHEESE, SOFTENED

1 OZ/25 G UNSALTED BUTTER, SOFTENED

8 OZ/225 G BLUE STILTON, ROUGHLY CRUMBLED

2 TBSP/30 ML PORT

1 LARGE FIRM PEAR, PEELED, CORED AND ROUGHLY CHOPPED

1 TBSP/15ML CHOPPED CELERY LEAVES

PEPPER

TO SERVE

2 HEADS CELERY, TRIMMED AND WASHED

═══

◇ Beat together the cream cheese, butter and half the stilton, until smooth and creamy.

◇ Stir in the remaining ingredients and press into a transportable dish. Cover and chill for several hours.

◇ Serve straight from the dish, with the celery.

BACK *Watercress and herb soup*
FRONT *Potted stilton with port and pear*

CRAB & MANGO FILO PASTRIES

~

An exotic combination of crabmeat and mango make a wonderful savoury filling for these filo pastry parcels. If using canned crabmeat, drain well before mixing in.

FILLING

1 TBSP/15 ML OLIVE OIL

3 SPRING ONIONS, TRIMMED AND FINELY CHOPPED

1 CLOVE GARLIC, CRUSHED

2 TSP/10 ML CHOPPED FRESH CORIANDER

6 OZ/175 G FRESH OR CANNED WHITE CRABMEAT

2 OZ/50 G CURD CHEESE

1 SMALL MANGO, PEELED, STONED AND DICED

PINCH OF GROUND MIXED SPICE

PINCH OF CAYENNE PEPPER

SALT AND PEPPER

PASTRY

4 LARGE SHEETS FILO PASTRY

2 OZ/50 G UNSALTED BUTTER, MELTED

◇ Heat the oil and sauté the onion and garlic for 5 minutes. Cool and mix with all the remaining filling ingredients. Season to taste.
◇ Cut the pastry into 12 strips, 3½×14 in/9×35 cm, and keep covered with a clean tea-towel.
◇ Brush 1 strip with butter and place a heaped tablespoon of filling at one end. Fold over diagonally to form a triangle and continue folding on the diagonal, from side to side to the end of the pastry. Press the ends to seal and brush with butter.
◇ Repeat to make 12 triangular-shaped pastries. Place on a lightly greased baking tray and bake in a preheated oven at 200°C/400°F/gas mark 6 for 25 minutes, until golden.
◇ Leave to go cold on a wire rack and pack carefully in an airtight container.

THAI-STYLE PRAWN EGGS

~

A purée of prawns and soy sauce is pressed around small hard-boiled eggs, coated with sesame seeds and deep-fried, to make this Thai-style savoury snack.

6 SMALL EGGS (SIZE 5)

1 LB/450 G PEELED PRAWNS

4 SPRING ONIONS, TRIMMED AND CHOPPED

2 OZ/50 G FRESH WHITE BREADCRUMBS

1 SMALL CLOVE GARLIC, CRUSHED

1 TBSP/15 ML CHOPPED FRESH CORIANDER

2 TSP/10 ML SOY SAUCE

1 TSP/5ML GRATED FRESH ROOT GINGER

COATING

A LITTLE PLAIN FLOUR

1 EGG, LIGHTLY BEATEN

2-3 OZ/50-75 G SESAME SEEDS

OIL FOR DEEP FRYING

◇ Boil the eggs for 12 minutes, plunge immediately into cold water and leave to go cold before peeling.
◇ Purée the prawns in a food processor. Add the onions, breadcrumbs, garlic, coriander, soy sauce and ginger and purée together until smooth.
◇ Form the mixture into 6 balls, flatten each one out to a 4 in/10 cm round. Place a hard-boiled egg in the centre of each round, then press the mixture around the egg to completely enclose it. Coat lightly in a little flour, dip into the beaten egg and then into the sesame seeds, until well coated. Chill for 15 minutes.
◇ Heat 4 in/10 cm of oil in a heavy based pan, to a temperature of 180°C/350°F. Deep-fry the prawn eggs in batches, for 2-3 minutes each, until lightly golden. Drain on kitchen paper and leave to go cold.

FRONT *Crab and mango filo pastries*
BACK *Thai-style prawn eggs*

DOLMADES

~

These savoury stuffed vine leaves are a national dish of both Greece and Turkey. The fillings vary slightly, depending on where they are made. This is my particular favourite. Fresh vine leaves can be used, when available. Blanch them in boiling salted water for a few seconds to soften them slightly before use.

FILLING

2 TBSP/30 ML OLIVE OIL

6 OZ/175 G LONG GRAIN RICE, WASHED

1 OZ/25 G PINE NUTS

1 OZ/25 G CURRANTS

1 TBSP/15 ML CHOPPED FRESH MINT

1 TSP/5 ML SUGAR

1 TSP/5 ML GROUND CUMIN

¼ TSP/1.25 ML GROUND CINNAMON

3 FLOZ/75 ML WATER

1 TBSP/15 ML LEMON JUICE

STOCK

JUICE OF 1 LEMON

2 TBSP/30 ML OLIVE OIL

WATER

TO SERVE

LEMON WEDGES

YOGURT

◇ Wash the drained vine leaves, pat dry and sort out 18 good-sized leaves. Use the remaining leaves to line a 7 in/18 cm square ovenproof dish. Set aside.
◇ Prepare the filling: heat the oil and stir-fry the rice for 1 minute, until transparent. Stir in the remaining ingredients, cover and simmer very gently for 10 minutes. Transfer to a bowl and leave to cool.
◇ Place 2 tsp/10 ml of the rice mixture in the centre of a vine leaf. Fold the bottom of the leaf over the filling, then fold in the sides and finally roll up to the top of the leaf, to form a small log-shaped parcel. Repeat to make 18 dolmades. Place in the prepared dish, to fit tightly together.
◇ Put the lemon juice and oil in a measuring jug and make up to ½ pint/300 ml with water. Pour over the dolmades and bake in a preheated oven at 180°C/350°F/gas mark 4 for 1¼ hours, adding extra water if necessary.
◇ Leave to cool in the dish. Serve with lemon wedges and natural yogurt.

FETA, WALNUT & ONION DIP

~

A tangy, lightly spiced and fruited cheese dip. Serve with pitta bread and a selection of vegetable crudités.

7 OZ/200 G PACKET FETA CHEESE, DRAINED

4 TBSP/60 ML GREEK YOGURT

2 OZ/50 G CHOPPED WALNUTS

1 OZ/25 G DRIED FIGS, CHOPPED

1 SMALL CLOVE GARLIC, CRUSHED

1 TBSP/15 ML CHOPPED FRESH DILL

1 TSP/5 ML GROUND CINNAMON

PINCH OF GROUND NUTMEG

½ RED ONION, CHOPPED

◇ Crumble the feta into a bowl and beat in the yogurt, until combined.
◇ Stir in all the remaining ingredients, cover and chill until required.

BACK LEFT *Dolmades*
FRONT *Feta, walnut and onion dip*

PASTA, HAM & APRICOT SALAD

~

Making your own mayonnaise is surprisingly simple with the use of a food processor or blender. Commercially made mayonnaise can be substituted if you are short of time, in which case, add the strained oil and curry powder to 3 floz/75 ml of prepared mayonnaise and continue as the recipe directs.

8 OZ/225 G DRIED PASTA SHAPES

MAYONNAISE

3 TBSP/45 ML OLIVE OIL

1 SMALL ONION, CHOPPED

2 TSP/10 ML CURRY POWDER

LIGHT OLIVE OIL

1 EGG YOLK

1 TSP/5 ML LEMON JUICE

SALT AND PEPPER

6 OZ/175 G PIECE THICKLY SLICED HAM

6 OZ/175 G FRESH APRICOTS

1 ORANGE PEPPER

2 OZ/50 G CASHEW NUTS, TOASTED

◇ Cook the pasta in boiling salted water, with 1 tsp/5 ml oil, for 10-12 minutes until 'al dente' (just done). Drain, refresh under cold water to prevent further cooking, and leave to go cold.
◇ For the mayonnaise: heat the 3 tbsp/45 ml olive oil and sauté the onion and curry powder for 3 minutes. Strain into a measuring jug and make up to 7 floz/200 ml with light olive oil.
◇ Blend the egg yolk, lemon juice, salt and pepper in a food processor or blender, and with the blade running, pour in the oil in a steady stream, through the funnel, until the mixture becomes thick and creamy. If too thick, thin the mayonnaise with boiling water. Cover and set aside.
◇ Cut the ham into short strips. Stone and slice the apri-cots and de-seed and slice the pepper. Place in a large bowl and toss in the pasta, until combined.
◇ Stir in 4-5 tbsp/60-75 ml mayonnaise and sprinkle over the nuts just before serving.

MINTED LAMB CUTLETS

~

Lamb cutlets are marinated and then grilled, and the marinade is reduced with onion, vinegar and sugar to make a tangy relish.

12 LAMB CUTLETS

MARINADE

6 TBSP/90 ML OLIVE OIL

6 TBSP/90 ML DRY WHITE WINE

4 TBSP/60 ML CHOPPED FRESH MINT

RELISH

1 LARGE ONION, VERY FINELY CHOPPED

2 TBSP/30 ML WHITE WINE VINEGAR

1 TBSP/15 ML SUGAR

SALT AND PEPPER

TO GARNISH

MINT LEAVES

◇ Wash the cutlets, pat dry and season with salt and pep-per. Place in a large shallow dish.
◇ Blend the marinade ingredients together and pour over the cutlets. Cover and marinate in the refrigerator for several hours, turning occasionally.
◇ Remove the cutlets from the marinade and place under a hot grill for 4-5 minutes on each side. Leave to go cold.
◇ Meanwhile, make the relish: put the onion, vinegar and sugar into a heavy based saucepan, add the marinade and simmer over a medium heat for 10 minutes. Leave to go cold. Store in a screw-top jar.

TOP *Pasta, ham and apricot salad*
BOTTOM *Minted lamb cutlets*

GORGONZOLA &
ASPARAGUS QUICHE

~

The classic combination of asparagus and blue cheese works particularly well in this savoury quiche with the gorgonzola adding a rich creaminess to the filling. (Dolcelatte is a good alternative to gorgonzola.)

PASTRY

6 OZ/175 G PLAIN FLOUR

1 OZ/25 G FRESHLY GRATED PARMESAN CHEESE

PINCH OF SALT

4 OZ/100 G UNSALTED BUTTER, DICED

1 EGG YOLK

1 TBSP/15 ML COLD WATER

FILLING

8 OZ/225 G ASPARAGUS SPEARS

4 OZ/100 G GORGONZOLA CHEESE, CRUMBLED

1 TBSP/15 ML CHOPPED FRESH BASIL

7 FLOZ/200 ML SINGLE CREAM

3 EGGS, LIGHTLY BEATEN

2 TBSP/30 ML FRESHLY GRATED PARMESAN CHEESE

SALT AND PEPPER

◇ Make the pastry: combine the flour, cheese and salt in a large bowl, and rub in the butter until the mixture resembles fine breadcrumbs. Work in the egg yolk and water to form a firm paste. Wrap and chill for 20 minutes.
◇ Roll out the pastry and use to line a 9 in/23 cm fluted flan tin. Prick the base and chill for 15 minutes.
◇ Bake blind in a preheated oven at 200°C/400°F/gas mark 6 for 8 minutes, remove the beans and foil and return to the oven for a further 12-15 minutes, until the pastry is crisp and lightly golden. Cool slightly.
◇ Trim the asparagus and blanch in boiling water for 2 minutes. Drain, refresh under cold water, and pat dry. Reserve 8 tips and chop the remainder.

◇ Sprinkle the chopped asparagus, Gorgonzola and basil into the pastry case, beat together the cream and eggs and pour over. Arrange the asparagus tips attractively over the filling and sprinkle with the Parmesan.
◇ Lower the oven temperature to 190°C/375°F/gas mark 5 and bake for 25-30 minutes, until golden and set.

BEETROOT, TARRAGON
& GINGER SALAD

~

In my opinion, beetroot is a much underrated vegetable. If you have time, cook the beets yourself for this recipe: bake them for 1½–2 hours at 180°C/350°F/gas mark 4, loosely covered with foil.

2 LB/900 G COOKED BEETROOT (SEE ABOVE)

DRESSING

4 TBSP/60 ML HAZELNUT OIL

1 TBSP/15 ML BALSAMIC VINEGAR

2 TSP/10 ML CHOPPED FRESH TARRAGON

1 TSP/5 ML GRATED FRESH ROOT GINGER

SALT AND PEPPER

TO SERVE

1 BUNCH SPRING ONIONS, TRIMMED AND THICKLY SLICED

2 OZ/50 G HAZELNUTS, TOASTED

TO GARNISH

TARRAGON SPRIGS (OPTIONAL)

◇ Peel the cooked beetroot if necessary, and cut into wedges. Place in a plastic container.
◇ Blend the dressing ingredients together and pour over the beetroot. Toss well, cover and leave to infuse.
◇ Toss with the onions and sprinkle over the hazelnuts just before serving.

TOP *Gorgonzola and asparagus quiche*
BOTTOM *Beetroot, tarragon and ginger salad*

SALMON & DILL FLAN

~

*Flans are always popular on picnics. This particularly
pretty one tastes as good as it looks.*

═══

PASTRY

7 OZ/200 G PLAIN FLOUR

½ TSP/2.5 ML SALT

4 OZ/100 G UNSALTED BUTTER, DICED

1 EGG YOLK

1 TBSP/15 ML COLD WATER

FILLING

8 OZ/225 G SMOKED SALMON

3 EGGS

½ PINT/300 ML SOURED CREAM

3 TBSP/45 ML CHOPPED FRESH DILL

1 TBSP/15 ML WHOLEGRAIN MUSTARD

1 TBSP/15 ML LEMON JUICE

PEPPER

═══

◇ Make the pastry: sift the flour and salt together into a
bowl and rub in the butter until the mixture resembles fine
breadcrumbs. Make a well in the centre and work in the
egg yolk and water to form a firm paste. Wrap and chill for
30 minutes.

◇ Roll out the dough on a lightly floured surface and use
to line a deep 9 in/23 cm fluted flan tin. Prick the base
with a fork and chill for a further 15 minutes.

◇ Bake blind in a preheated oven at 200°C/400°F/gas
mark 6 for 10 minutes. Remove the beans and foil and
bake for a further 10-12 minutes, until the pastry is crisp
and lightly golden. Remove the flan case from the oven
and leave to cool.

◇ Roughly chop the salmon and sprinkle over the cooled
pastry case. Beat the remaining ingredients together until
combined, and pour over the salmon.

◇ Bake the flan for 25 minutes until golden and firm in
the centre. Remove from the oven and leave to cool.

◇ Transport the flan in its tin and serve cut into wedges.

SMOKED TROUT PASTE

~

*Serve this creamy trout paste with a selection of
crackers or a French stick.*

═══

8 OZ/225 G SMOKED TROUT FILLETS

4 OZ/100 G RICOTTA OR CURD CHEESE

2 TBSP/30 ML CREAMED HORSERADISH SAUCE

1 TBSP/15 ML CHOPPED FRESH CHIVES

1 TBSP/15 ML BRANDY (OPTIONAL)

JUICE OF 1 LEMON

2 TBSP/30 ML SINGLE CREAM OR
FROMAGE FRAIS

PEPPER

═══

◇ Roughly chop the trout and purée in a food processor
with all the remaining ingredients, except the cream, until
smooth. Stir in the cream and adjust seasoning.

◇ Transfer to a container and chill until required.

◇ Serve with slices of French stick or crackers.

LEFT *Salmon and dill flan*
RIGHT *Smoked trout paste*

COUNTRY CHICKEN, HAM & HERB TERRINE

~

A rich chicken and herb mousse is layered alternately with strips of ham and whole chicken breast, set, and unmoulded to reveal an array of herbs.

12 OZ/375 G PIECE THICKLY SLICED HAM

1½ LB/675 G CHICKEN BREAST FILLETS, SKINNED

½ PINT/300 ML CHICKEN STOCK

1 TBSP/15 ML OLIVE OIL

1 SMALL ONION, MINCED

1 CLOVE GARLIC, CRUSHED

1 EGG, SEPARATED

JUICE OF 1 LEMON

PINCH OF GROUND MIXED SPICE

¼ PINT/150 ML DOUBLE CREAM

0.4 OZ/11 G PACKET POWDERED GELATINE

2 OZ/50 G SHELLED PISTACHIO NUTS

2 TBSP/30 ML CHOPPED HERBS (PARSLEY, TARRAGON, THYME)

SALT AND PEPPER

TO GARNISH

A SELECTION OF PRETTY HERBS

◇ Trim fat from ham and cut into ¼ in/0.5 cm strips.
◇ Poach 2 chicken breasts in the stock for 12-15 minutes. Drain and cool. Reserve 3 tbsp/45 ml of stock.
◇ Finely chop the remaining chicken. Heat the oil and sauté the chopped chicken with the onion and garlic for 6-8 minutes, until cooked. Leave to cool.
◇ Lightly oil a 2 lb/900 g loaf tin, and lay fresh herbs over the base, pressing them down lightly. Set aside.
◇ Purée the chicken and onion with the egg yolk, lemon juice, mixed spice and salt and pepper until very smooth. Turn into a bowl and stir in the cream.
◇ Heat the gelatine gently in the reserved poaching stock until dissolved. Stir in a spoonful of chicken purée, then stir the gelatine mixture into the remaining purée. Stir in the nuts and chopped herbs.
◇ Whisk the egg white until stiff and fold into the chicken mixture, until incorporated. Spoon a shallow layer of the chicken mousse mixture into the base of the prepared tin, spreading very carefully over the herbs without moving them. Layer the strips of ham, chicken breast and chicken mousse into the tin, finishing with the mousse. Tap to dislodge holes, smooth and chill until set.

SUMMER LEAF SALAD

~

Use a selection of your favourite salad leaves and herbs for this light and fragrant salad.

DRESSING

4 TBSP/60 ML EXTRA VIRGIN OLIVE OIL

2 TSP/10 ML RASPBERRY OR OTHER FRUIT VINEGAR

1 TSP/5 ML WHOLEGRAIN MUSTARD

½ TSP/2.5 ML TSP CLEAR HONEY

SALT AND PEPPER

SALAD

6 LARGE HANDFULS OF MIXED SUMMER LEAVES (COS, FRISÉE [CURLY ENDIVE], LOLLO ROSSO, MACHE, OAK LEAF, RADDICCHIO, ROCKET)

6 TBSP/90 ML CHOPPED HERBS (BASIL, CHERVIL, CHIVES, LEMON, BALM, MINT, TARRAGON, THYME)

2 TBSP/30 ML SUNFLOWER SEEDS, TOASTED

EDIBLE FLOWERS (BORAGE, NASTURTIUM FLOWERS, PANSIES, ROSE PETALS, VIOLAS)

◇ Blend the dressing ingredients together, and place in a screw-top jar. Mix all the salad ingredients together in a large bowl, shake the dressing to amalgamate the oil and vinegar, and pour over the salad. Scatter over the flowers, toss well and serve immediately.

TOP *Country chicken, ham and herb terrine*
BOTTOM *Summer leaf salad*

PISSALADIÈRE

~

Try this tasty variation of the classic Niçoise pizza. The dough is spread with olive paste and topped with sweet onions, anchovies, thyme and olives. Olive paste is available from most good supermarkets and delicatessens.

═══

TOPPING

2 TBSP/30 ML OLIVE OIL

1½ LB/675 G ONIONS, THINLY SLICED

2 CLOVES GARLIC, CRUSHED

1 TBSP/15 ML CHOPPED FRESH THYME

1 TSP/5 ML FENNEL SEEDS

2 OZ/50 G CAN ANCHOVY FILLETS, DRAINED

A LITTLE MILK

1 TBSP/15 ML OLIVE PASTE

8-12 PITTED BLACK OLIVES

DOUGH

8 OZ/225 G PLAIN FLOUR

1 TSP/5 ML FAST-ACTING DRIED YEAST

½ TSP/2.5 ML SALT

2 TBSP/30 ML OLIVE OIL

4 FLOZ-¼ PINT/125-150 ML TEPID WATER

GLAZE

1 EGG YOLK, BEATEN WITH 1 TBSP/15 ML MILK
AND A PINCH OF SALT

═══

◇ Heat the oil and sauté the onions, garlic, thyme, and fennel seeds for 20-25 minutes, until the onions are softened and lightly golden. Stir from time to time to stop the onions from burning, as they will become bitter.

◇ Soak the anchovy fillets in a little milk for 10 minutes, to remove the saltiness, drain and pat dry. Set aside.

◇ Prepare the dough: combine the flour, yeast and salt in a large bowl, make a well in the centre and work in the oil and enough warm water to form a pliable dough. Knead on a lightly floured surface for 5 minutes, until smooth and elastic. Place the dough in a lightly oiled bowl, brush the surface with oil and cover with polythene. Leave to rise in a warm place until doubled in size.

◇ Knock the dough back and roll out on a lightly floured surface to a 10 in/25 cm round and place on a greased baking tray or pizza plate. Prick the base with a fork.

◇ Spread the dough with the olive paste and top with the onion mixture, anchovies and olives. With a sharp knife, cut small slits all around the edge of the dough to make an attractive finish. Brush with a little glaze and drizzle the onion mixture with oil and bake in a preheated oven at 240°C/475°F/gas mark 9 for 25 minutes, until golden.

◇ Allow to go cold and serve cut into wedges, with a spoonful of crème fraîche, if wished.

◇ For a tasty alternative, substitute the anchovy fillets with 1 oz/25 g drained, sun-dried tomatoes in oil.

Pissaladière

BEEF & HERB ROULADE

~

This is my version of the Sicilian dish Farso Magro, a rolled, stuffed rump steak, served cold cut into slices. This recipe serves 8 – 10. Ask your butcher to cut you a steak from the widest part of the rump.

1×2 LB/900 G RUMP STEAK

FILLING

6 OZ/175 G PARMA HAM, SLICED THICKLY

12 OZ/375 G LEAN MINCED BEEF

2 CLOVES GARLIC, CRUSHED

2 OZ/50 G PITTED GREEN OLIVES

3 TBSP/45 ML FRESHLY GRATED PARMESAN CHEESE

2 OZ/50 G FRESH WHITE BREADCRUMBS

2 TBSP/30 ML CHOPPED FRESH HERBS (BASIL, OREGANO, SAGE AND THYME)

1 TBSP/15 ML CAPERS, FINELY CHOPPED

2 SMALL EGGS, LIGHTLY BEATEN

SALT AND PEPPER

2 TBSP/30 ML OLIVE OIL

◇ Trim any fat from the steak and place between 2 sheets of waxed paper. Beat gently with a rolling pin to flatten to ½ in/1 cm thick. Discard the paper and cover the steak with the slices of ham.
◇ Mix all the remaining ingredients together, except the oil, seasoning well. Spread the mixture over the ham, leaving a narrow border round the edge of the steak.
◇ Roll up the steak from one long side, tucking the ends under as you go, to seal in the filling. Tie up with string securely, but not too tightly.
◇ Heat the oil in a large frying pan and brown the beef on all sides. Wrap loosely in foil, place in a roasting pan and cook in a preheated oven at 200°C/400°F/gas mark 6 for 1 hour. Remove from the oven and leave in the foil until cold.
◇ Wrap in waxed paper and transport in a cool box.

ONION & PEPPER RELISH

~

An excellent accompaniment to cold meats and pies, which can be made in advance and stored in a screw-top jar.

1 LARGE RED PEPPER

8 OZ/225 G PICKLING ONIONS

1 TBSP/15 ML OLIVE OIL

2 CLOVES GARLIC, PEELED

1 TSP/5 ML MUSTARD SEEDS

1 TSP/5 ML CHOPPED FRESH THYME

1 CINNAMON STICK

6 WHOLE CLOVES

3 FLOZ/75 ML WATER

2 TBSP/30 ML TOMATO PURÉE

2 TBSP/30 ML BALSAMIC VINEGAR

2 TBSP/30 ML SUGAR

1 BAYLEAF

½ TSP/2.5 ML SALT

PEPPER

◇ Place the pepper under a hot grill until the skin becomes charred and blistered, turning frequently. Wrap in a plastic bag and leave to cool for 30 minutes.
◇ Blanch the onions in boiling water for 1 minute. Drain, then refresh under cold water. Peel and cut in half.
◇ Heat the oil in a heavy based pan and fry the onions, garlic, mustard seeds and thyme for 5 minutes, until the onions are brown. Add the remaining ingredients, cover and simmer for 10 minutes.
◇ Peel the cooled pepper over a bowl to catch any juices. Discard the seeds. Cut the flesh into thin strips and add to the pan with the juices.
◇ Remove the pan from the heat and leave the relish to go cold. Spoon into a screw-top jar and store in a cool place.

LEFT *Beef and herb roulade*
RIGHT *Onion and pepper relish*

PEAR & CARDAMOM TATIN

~

*This wickedly delicious upside-down pie is best eaten
the same day, with a spoonful of crème fraîche.*

══

PASTRY

6 OZ/175 G PLAIN FLOUR

½ TSP/2.5 ML SALT

6 OZ/175 G UNSALTED BUTTER, DICED

1 OZ/25 G WALNUTS, FINELY GROUND

2 TSP/10 ML CASTER SUGAR

1 EGG YOLK

CARAMEL

3 OZ/75 G UNSALTED BUTTER

3 OZ/75 G CASTER SUGAR

3 CARDAMOM PODS

TOPPING

3 LB/1.5 KG FIRM PEARS, PEELED, HALVED
AND CORED

1 OZ/25 G WALNUT HALVES

══

◇ To make the pastry, sift the flour and salt into a large
bowl. Rub in the butter until the mixture resembles fine
breadcrumbs. Stir in the walnuts and sugar and work in
the egg yolk and 1 tbsp/15 ml cold water to form a soft
dough. Wrap and chill for 20 minutes.
◇ Melt the butter and sugar in an 8-9 in/20-23 cm ovenproof frying pan. Remove seeds from the cardamom pods,
crush them and add to the pan. Boil for 5 minutes. Add the
pears, cut side up. Cook for 5 minutes, or until the pears
begin to brown underneath. Add walnut halves.
◇ Roll out the chilled pastry to a circle a little larger than
the pan. Cover the pears with the pastry, pressing it up the
sides of the pan.
◇ Transfer to a preheated oven at 200°C/400°F/gas
mark 6 and bake for 20 minutes, until golden.
◇ Leave in the pan for 5 minutes and invert on to a large
plate. Leave to go cold.

CARAMELIZED ORANGES

~

*Whole fresh oranges are served with a boozy citrus
sauce and decorated with ripe cherries to make this
attractive chilled summer dessert.*

══

8 LARGE ORANGES

6 OZ/175 G GRANULATED SUGAR

3 FL OZ/75 ML WATER

JUICE OF 1 LEMON

6 OZ/175 G CHERRIES ON STALKS

2 TBSP/30 ML GRAND MARNIER

TO DECORATE

LEMON BALM LEAVES

══

◇ Peel 6 of the oranges, removing all the pith, and set
aside. Peel the 2 remaining oranges, leaving the pith on,
and cut the peel into thin strips. Blanch the strips in boiling water for 2 minutes, drain, refresh under cold water
and pat dry. Halve the 2 semi-peeled oranges and squeeze
the juice into a bowl.
◇ Heat the sugar gently until dissolved, add the water,
orange juice and lemon juice and boil rapidly for 3
minutes until thick and syrupy. Add the peeled oranges to
the pan, turning them to coat them with syrup. Remove
the oranges to a shallow dish, surround them with the
cherries, and set aside to cool.
◇ Add the shredded peel to the syrup and boil rapidly for
4-5 minutes, until the peel begins to caramelize. Remove
from the heat and pour in the Grand Marnier.
◇ Pour the syrup and caramelized shreds over the
oranges and cherries. Leave to go cold and chill for several
hours or overnight, spooning over the sauce occasionally.
◇ Serve decorated with lemon balm leaves if wished.

TOP *Pear and cardamom tatin*
BOTTOM *Caramelized oranges*

LEMON CHEESECAKE WITH SUMMER BERRY SAUCE

~

A tangy lemon cheesecake made with a low-fat soft cheese and fromage frais. A purée of summer berries makes the perfect sauce.

BASE

5 OZ/150 G DIGESTIVE BISCUITS, CRUSHED

2 OZ/50 G UNSALTED BUTTER, MELTED

FILLING

8 OZ/225 G LOW-FAT SOFT CHEESE

8 OZ/225 G FROMAGE FRAIS

3 OZ/75 G SUGAR

2 EGGS

RIND AND JUICE OF 1 LARGE LEMON

1 OZ/25 G PLAIN FLOUR

½ TSP GROUND MIXED SPICE

SAUCE

1 LB/450 G MIXED SUMMER BERRIES

1 OZ/25 G SUGAR

2 TBSP/30 ML CASSIS

TO DECORATE

SUMMER BERRIES

◇ Grease, and line the base and sides of a 7 in/18 cm spring-release cake tin.

◇ Make the base: stir the crushed biscuits into the melted butter until well coated, and press into the base of the prepared tin. Chill for 15 minutes.

◇ Meanwhile, prepare the filling: beat all the ingredients together until smooth. Pour the mixture over the chilled biscuit base and bake in a preheated oven at 180°C/350°F/gas mark 4 for 45-50 minutes, until just firm in the centre. Remove from the oven, cover with a clean tea-towel and leave to cool in the tin and chill.

◇ Make the sauce: reserve 4 oz/100 g mixed berries for decoration. Hull the strawberries and discard the stalks from the currants and wash all the fruit well. Place in a pan with the sugar and cassis and simmer gently for 5 minutes, until the fruit is soft. Purée until smooth and pass through a sieve to remove the seeds. Set aside to cool and transfer to a screw-top jar.

SPICED APPLE & BLUEBERRY MUFFINS

~

Quick to make, these American-style fruit muffins are delicious with crème fraîche or yogurt. This recipe makes 12 large muffins.

MUFFINS

8 OZ/225 G PLAIN FLOUR

1 TBSP/15 ML BAKING POWDER

3 OZ/75 G SUGAR

1 TSP/5 ML GROUND MIXED SPICE

PINCH OF SALT

4 OZ/100 G UNSALTED BUTTER, MELTED

1 EGG, LIGHTLY BEATEN

6 FLOZ/175 ML MILK

1 DESSERT APPLE, PEELED, CORED AND CHOPPED

3 OZ/75 G BLUEBERRIES

◇ Place the flour, baking powder, sugar, mixed spice, salt, butter, egg and milk in a food processor and blend until smooth.

◇ Transfer to a bowl and stir in the apple and blueberries until evenly combined. Spoon into a lightly oiled muffin tray and bake in a preheated oven at 220°C/425°F/gas mark 7 for 15-20 minutes, until risen and golden.

◇ Remove from the oven, cool in the tin for 5 minutes, and turn out on to a wire rack to go cold.

FRONT *Lemon cheesecake with summer berry sauce*
BACK *Spiced apple and blueberry muffins*

PEACH NECTAR

~

Crème de peche is a peach liqueur from France, and is quite delicious, especially when blended with chilled white wine and topped up with sparkling mineral water. You could substitute it with brandy, if unavailable, and stir in 1 tbsp/15 ml clear honey.

1×75 CL BOTTLE CHILLED DRY WHITE WINE

4 FLOZ/125 ML CRÈME DE PECHE

1 RIPE PEACH, STONED AND THINLY SLICED

1 PINT/600 ML SPARKLING MINERAL WATER

TO SERVE

ICE CUBES

◇ Pour the wine into a large jug, add the crème de peche and peach slices, and top up with the sparkling water.
◇ Add a few ice cubes and serve immediately.

RASPBERRY & GINGER CORDIAL

~

A deliciously refreshing summer cordial, colourful and fragrant, it makes the perfect non-alcoholic aperitif. If you prefer, use sparkling wine instead of mineral water.

CORDIAL

1 LB/450 G RASPBERRIES

6 TBSP/90 ML CLEAR HONEY

JUICE OF 1 LEMON

2 TSP/10 ML GROUND GINGER

TO SERVE

CRUSHED ICE

SPARKLING MINERAL WATER

◇ Purée the raspberries, honey, lemon juice and ginger together, in a food processor or blender, until smooth. Pass through a fine sieve to remove the pips.
◇ Pour into a screw-top jar or bottle and chill.
◇ Divide the cordial between 6 glasses, add crushed ice, and top up with mineral water. Serve immediately.

SOUTHERN MINT JULEP

~

A deliciously refreshing minted whiskey cocktail. Serve decorated with extra mint leaves.

MINT SYRUP

1 LARGE LEMON

1 TBSP/15 ML SUGAR

6 SPRIGS MINT, BRUISED

½ PINT/300 ML BOILING WATER

TO SERVE

A HANDFUL MINT LEAVES, CRUSHED

6 TBSP/90 ML WHISKEY

6 TSP/30 ML ICING SUGAR

CRUSHED ICE

MINT SPRIGS (OPTIONAL)

◇ Make the syrup: slice the lemon thickly and place in a bowl with the sugar and mint sprigs. Pour in the boiling water and leave to infuse for 4 hours or overnight.
◇ Strain into a screw-top jar or bottle and keep cool.
◇ To serve: place 2 tbsp/30 ml of mint syrup into each glass and add a few crushed mint leaves, 1 tbsp/15 ml whiskey, and 1 tsp/5ml icing sugar to each one. Top up with crushed ice, stir well and decorate with mint sprigs.

RIGHT *Peach nectar*
LEFT *Raspberry and ginger cordial*
CENTRE *Southern mint julep*

DINING ALFRESCO

The recipes in this chapter are among the most elaborate; as the food is designed to be served outside at home, it will be easier for you to prepare more lavish dishes. At the same time it is important that you should be able to spend time outside with your guests, rather than slaving over the food in the kitchen, and the recipes have been carefully composed with this in mind. Most of the dishes can be prepared in advance and are served cold, and others, that are served warm or hot, only need to be popped into the oven or under the grill at the last moment. As you are close to the kitchen, there is no need to worry about transporting the food, but do make room in the refrigerator for any food that needs to be kept cool until it is required. This can be an occasion to use your most elegant china, glasses, cutlery and linen, but it will be just as enjoyable to relax around an informal table, and simply relish a selection of delicious and imaginative recipes in the open air. The recipes have been set out to make it easy to assemble a complete menu of fresh-tasting dishes that will provide a truly memorable alfresco lunch or dinner party.

CONTENTS

SMOKED SALMON FILO TARTLETS

~

A salad of smoked salmon, asparagus tips, hard-boiled eggs and rocket, served in filo pastry cases with a piquant shallot dressing, makes an attractive and elegant starter.

1×10 OZ/300 G PACKET FILO PASTRY SHEETS

2 OZ/50 G UNSALTED BUTTER, MELTED

24 ASPARAGUS TIPS

5 SMALL EGGS, HARD BOILED

6 OZ/175 G SMOKED SALMON

2 OZ/50 G ROCKET

DRESSING

6 TBSP/90 ML EXTRA VIRGIN OLIVE OIL

3 TBSP/45 ML SOURED CREAM

4 TSP/20 ML SHERRY VINEGAR

1 TBSP/15 ML CHOPPED FRESH DILL

SALT AND PEPPER

TO GARNISH

DILL SPRIGS

◇ Cut the filo pastry into 24×5 in/13 cm squares.
◇ Lightly butter 6×4½ in/12 cm tartlet tins and lay 4 squares of pastry in each one, brushing the pastry with melted butter. Press gently into the edges to form 6 star-shaped filo pastry cases. The ends of the pastry will stick up above the tops of tins. Leave for 30 minutes to allow the pastry to firm up.
◇ Bake in a preheated oven at 180°C/350°F/gas mark 4 for 15-20 minutes, until crisp and golden. Cool slightly and carefully lift the pastry cases out of the tins and cool on a wire rack.
◇ Prepare the salad filling: blanch the asparagus tips in boiling water for 1 minute. Drain, refresh under cold water and pat dry.
◇ Peel and quarter the cooked eggs.

◇ Cut the salmon into thin strips.
◇ Wash and dry the rocket.
◇ Blend all the dressing ingredients together.
◇ Arrange the asparagus, eggs, salmon and rocket in the filo cases, spoon over the dressing, garnish and serve.

FRESH PEA & LETTUCE SOUP

~

A light and delicate summer soup that can be served hot or cold. If serving cold, leave the soup to cool, then stir in ¼ pint/150 ml natural yogurt and chill for 2 hours.

1 TBSP/15 ML OLIVE OIL

1 ONION, FINELY CHOPPED

1 MEDIUM ROUND LETTUCE

2 LB/900 G FRESH PEAS, SHELLED

2 TBSP/30 ML CHOPPED FRESH MINT

1¼ PINT/750 ML VEGETABLE STOCK

JUICE OF 1 LEMON

SALT AND PEPPER

TO GARNISH

A LITTLE NATURAL YOGURT

BASIL LEAVES

◇ Heat the oil and sauté the onion for 5 minutes.
◇ Wash and dry the lettuce, discarding any tough outer leaves, and slice thinly. Add to the pan with the peas and mint. Stir once and add the stock, lemon juice and seasonings. Bring to the boil, cover and simmer gently for 15-20 minutes, until the peas are cooked.
◇ Purée the soup in a food processor or blender and serve at once with a swirl of yogurt and basil leaves.

BACK *Smoked salmon filo tartlets*
FRONT *Fresh pea and lettuce soup*

RADICCHIO WITH GRILLED GOATS CHEESE

~

The slightly bitter flavour of the radicchio is complemented with the creamy, melted goats cheese and sweet char-grilled pepper.

═══

3 RED PEPPERS

6 OZ/175 G GOATS CHEESE

¼ PINT/150 ML HAZELNUT OIL

4 TSP/20 ML BALSAMIC VINEGAR

6 SPRIGS ROSEMARY, BRUISED

6 ROUNDS FRENCH BREAD

1 CLOVE GARLIC, HALVED

1 SMALL RADICCHIO

2 TBSP/30 ML HAZELNUTS, TOASTED AND CHOPPED

PEPPER

═══

◇ Place the peppers under a hot grill until the skins are charred and blistered, turning frequently. Remove from heat and place in a plastic bag for 30 minutes to soften.
◇ Cut the goats cheese into 6 thin slices and place in a shallow dish. Blend the oil and vinegar together and pour over the cheese. Add the rosemary, cover and leave to marinate for several hours.
◇ Trim the French bread to the same size as the cheese and toast lightly on both sides. Rub all over with the garlic and set aside.
◇ Peel the peppers over a bowl to catch the juices. Discard the seeds, cut the flesh into thick strips and set aside.
◇ Remove the cheese from the marinade and sit on top of the toasted bread. Discard all but 1 sprig of rosemary. Chop the leaves finely, then return to the oil and vinegar.
◇ Wash the radicchio and separate the leaves. Arrange a few leaves and the peppers on 6 serving plates.
◇ Grill the cheese croûtons for 1-2 minutes until the cheese just melts and place 1 on each plate. Drizzle over the marinade and sprinkle over the toasted hazelnuts.

PARMA SALAD

~

In this pretty salad starter, slices of parma ham and fresh figs are served with a mixture of ricotta and fresh herbs, formed into small egg shapes.

═══

SALAD

1 TBSP/15 ML CHOPPED FRESH HERBS (BASIL, FENNEL, OREGANO, TARRAGON)

½ CLOVE GARLIC, CRUSHED

8 OZ/225 G RICOTTA CHEESE

6 OZ/175 G PARMA HAM SLICES

6 RIPE FIGS

DRESSING

4 TBSP/60 ML EXTRA VIRGIN OLIVE OIL

1 TBSP/15 ML RASPBERRY OR OTHER FRUIT VINEGAR

PINCH OF SUGAR

SALT AND PEPPER

TO GARNISH

A SELECTION OF FRESH HERB LEAVES

═══

◇ Stir the herbs and garlic into the ricotta until combined. Using 2 teaspoons, pass a spoonful of the mixture from 1 to the other to form a small egg shape. Repeat to make 18 mounds. Chill until required.
◇ Cut each fig into 3 wedges.
◇ Arrange the slices of ham on a large serving plate and arrange the ricotta mounds and fig wedges attractively over the top.
◇ Blend the dressing ingredients together and drizzle over the salad. Garnish and serve at once.

FRONT *Radicchio with grilled goats cheese*
BACK *Parma salad*

SCALLOP & MUSSEL ESCABECHE

~

Escabeche is a dish of cooked fish or meat chilled and marinated in oil, vinegar, herbs and spices. This is an adaptation of a Spanish recipe. If possible serve this elegant starter in scallop shells.

===

POACHING LIQUID

1 TBSP/15 ML OLIVE OIL

1 SMALL ONION, CHOPPED

1 CLOVE GARLIC, CRUSHED

¼ PINT/150 ML DRY WHITE WINE

¼ PINT/150 ML WATER

GRATED RIND AND JUICE OF 1 LIME

2 SPRIGS ROSEMARY, BRUISED

12 LARGE SCALLOPS

MARINADE

3½ FLOZ/100 ML LIGHT OLIVE OIL

JUICE OF 1 LIME

1 TBSP/15 ML CHOPPED FRESH PARSLEY

2 TSP/10 ML CHOPPED FRESH ROSEMARY

1 TSP/5 ML CORIANDER SEEDS, CRUSHED

PINCH OF SUGAR

PINCH OF CAYENNE PEPPER

SALT AND PEPPER

18 RAW MUSSELS IN SHELLS, SCRUBBED

TO GARNISH

LIME SLICES

PARSLEY SPRIGS

===

◇ Heat the oil and sauté the onion and garlic for 5 minutes. Add the wine, water, lime rind and juice and rosemary. Bring to the boil and simmer gently, covered, for 10 minutes.

◇ Wash and dry the scallops and cut away the tough membrane. Slice each scallop in half, horizontally, and poach in the liquid, over a very low heat, for 1-2 minutes, until they become opaque. Do not over-cook or the scallops will be tough. Remove with a slotted spoon and transfer to a shallow dish. Reserve the poaching liquid.

◇ Blend all the marinade ingredients together and pour over the scallops.

◇ Strain the reserved poaching liquid and add 3 floz/75 ml to the scallops. Set aside to marinate.

◇ Reduce the remaining liquid in a large pan until only about 3 tbsp/45 ml remains. Add the mussels to the pan, cover and cook for 4-5 minutes, agitating the pan, until all the mussel shells are open and the mussels are cooked. Discard any that do not open.

◇ Carefully remove the mussels from their shells, reserving 18 half shells. Add the mussels to the scallops and leave to marinate for 1-2 hours or longer.

◇ Serve the scallops and mussels and marinade in individual dishes or scallop shells, sitting the mussels back in their half shells, if liked. Garnish with lime slices and parsley and serve with crusty bread.

Scallop and mussel escabeche

STUFFED ONIONS WITH SUN-DRIED TOMATOES

~

The intense flavour of the sun-dried tomatoes combined with creamy goats cheese and pinenuts, makes this a truly delicious stuffing, which can be prepared in advance.

3 LARGE RED ONIONS, UN-PEELED

FILLING

4 OZ/100 G SUN-DRIED TOMATOES IN OIL, DRAINED

4 OZ/100 G GOATS CHEESE

1 CLOVE GARLIC, CRUSHED

2 OZ/50 G FRESH WHITE BREADCRUMBS

1 OZ/25 G PINENUTS, TOASTED

1 TBSP/15 ML CHOPPED FRESH BASIL

1 TSP/5 ML CHOPPED FRESH THYME

1 EGG

SALT AND PEPPER

TO SERVE

SALAD GARNISH

CRÈME FRAÎCHE

◇ Place the unpeeled onions in a large pan and cover with cold water. Bring to the boil, and cook for 15 minutes, until tender. Drain the onions and cool.
◇ Prepare the filling: slice the tomatoes thinly and place in a large bowl. Cube the cheese and add to tomatoes with the remaining ingredients, except the egg and set aside.
◇ Cut the cooled onions in half, through the root and tip, and carefully cut out most of the flesh leaving 1 or 2 layers to keep the shape and form the empty shells.
◇ Discard half of the flesh, finely chop the rest and stir into the filling. Lightly beat the egg and stir into the filling. Spoon into the empty shells, packing the mixture in well, and place in a heatproof dish.
◇ Bake in a preheated oven at 200°C/400°F/gas mark 6 for 20-25 minutes, until bubbling and golden.
◇ Serve the onions hot, warm or cold as a starter.

WARM PASTA POMMODORO

~

This is an unusual pasta dish, in that the hot pasta is tossed in an uncooked tomato sauce and served while still warm. This gives a wonderfully fresh tasting sauce, ideal for a summer evening.

3 LB/1.5 KG RIPE TOMATOES

2 OZ/50 G SUN-DRIED TOMATOES IN OIL, DRAINED AND THINLY SLICED

2 OZ/50 G PITTED BLACK OLIVES, HALVED

GRATED RIND AND JUICE OF 1 LEMON

2 TBSP/30 ML CHOPPED FRESH BASIL

¼ PINT/150 ML VIRGIN OLIVE OIL

1 LB 2 OZ/500 G FRESH LINGUINE OR TAGLIATELLE

1 CLOVE GARLIC, CHOPPED

1 SMALL DRIED RED CHILLI, DE-SEEDED AND CRUSHED

1 TSP/5 ML CHOPPED FRESH THYME

2 OZ/50 G CHOPPED WALNUTS, TOASTED

SALT AND PEPPER

TO GARNISH

BASIL LEAVES

◇ Peel and de-seed the tomatoes and chop the flesh. Place in a large bowl and stir in the sun-dried tomatoes, olives, lemon rind and juice, basil and 2 tbsp/30 ml olive oil. Cover and set aside to infuse for 1-2 hours.
◇ Just before serving, cook the pasta in plenty of boiling salted water for 2-3 minutes, until 'al dente' (just done).
◇ Meanwhile, heat the remaining oil in a large frying pan and sauté the garlic, chilli and thyme until golden. Remove the pan from the heat.
◇ Drain the cooked pasta and toss with the oil and garlic. Stir in the tomato sauce and walnuts and serve immediately, garnished with basil leaves and sprinkled with Parmesan if wished.

RIGHT *Stuffed onions with sun-dried tomatoes*
LEFT *Warm pasta pommodoro*

SPINACH & RICOTTA TART

PASTRY

6 OZ/175 G PLAIN FLOUR

1 OZ/25 G FRESHLY GRATED PARMESAN

PINCH OF SALT

4 OZ/100 G BUTTER, DICED

1 EGG YOLK

FILLING

1 TBSP/15 ML OLIVE OIL

2 LEEKS, TRIMMED AND THINLY SLICED

1 CLOVE GARLIC, CRUSHED

1 TBSP/15 ML CHOPPED FRESH THYME

8 OZ/225 G SPINACH LEAVES, SHREDDED

8 OZ/225 G RICOTTA CHEESE

3 EGGS, LIGHTLY BEATEN

¼ PINT/150 ML SINGLE CREAM

PINCH OF FRESHLY GRATED NUTMEG

1 OZ/25 G PINENUTS

SALT AND PEPPER

◇ Combine the flour, Parmesan and salt in a bowl and rub in the butter. Work in the egg yolk and 1 tbsp/15 ml cold water to form a firm paste. Wrap and chill for 30 minutes.

◇ Roll out the pastry and use to line a 9 in/23 cm fluted flan tin and prick the base. Chill for a further 15 minutes.

◇ Bake blind in a preheated oven at 200°C/400°F/gas mark 6 for 8 minutes. Remove the baking beans and foil and cook for a further 10-12 minutes, until the pastry is crisp and golden. Remove from the oven and leave to cool. Reduce oven temperature to 190°C/375°F/gas mark 5.

◇ Heat the oil in a large frying pan and sauté the leeks, garlic and thyme for 5 minutes. Add the spinach and stir for 1-2 minutes. Leave to cool slightly.

◇ Cream together the ricotta, eggs and cream until smooth and stir in the seasonings.

◇ Drain the spinach mixture, pressing out as much liquid as possible, and spread over the pastry case. Pour in the cheese mixture and sprinkle over the nuts. Bake for 30-35 minutes until lightly golden and set.

WATERCRESS ROULADE WITH SMOKED HADDOCK

8 OZ/225 G SMOKED HADDOCK FILLETS

½ PINT/300 ML MILK

8 OZ/225 G WATERCRESS

2 OZ/50 G BUTTER

2 OZ/50 G PLAIN FLOUR

3 EGGS, SEPARATED

2 OZ/50 G GRUYÈRE CHEESE, GRATED

FILLING

7 OZ/200 G CREAM CHEESE

2 TBSP/30 ML CHOPPED FRESH HERBS

1 OZ/25 G GROUND ALMONDS

1 OZ/25 G PARMESAN, GRATED

1 TBSP/15 ML LEMON JUICE

½ TSP/2.5 ML GROUND MACE

SALT AND PEPPER

◇ Line a 9×13 in/23×33 cm Swiss roll tin.

◇ Poach the haddock fillets in the milk for 6-8 minutes, until cooked. Drain and reserve the fish and stock.

◇ Wash and dry the watercress and discard the stalks. Chop finely and place in a large bowl.

◇ Melt the butter, stir in the flour and cook for 1 minute. Gradually add the stock and cook, stirring until thickened.

◇ Remove from the heat, cool slightly and beat in the egg yolks and cheese. Blend with the watercress and season.

◇ Whisk the egg whites until stiff and fold into the mixture, until combined. Spoon into the prepared tin, smooth the surface and bake in a preheated oven at 200°C/400°F/gas mark 6 for 20-25 minutes, until risen and set. Remove from the oven, cover with a clean tea-towel and cool.

◇ Skin and flake the haddock, and blend with the cream cheese and all remaining ingredients. When the roulade is cold, turn it out onto the tea-towel, peel off the paper and spread over the filling. Roll up tightly and serve sliced.

TOP *Spinach and ricotta tart*
BOTTOM *Watercress roulade with smoked haddock*

SPICED CHICKEN WITH TABBOULEH MOULDS

═══

1½ LB/675 G SKINLESS CHICKEN BREAST

2 TBSP/30 ML OLIVE OIL

1 CLOVE GARLIC, CRUSHED

1 TSP/5 ML GROUND CUMIN

½ TSP/2.5 ML GROUND MIXED SPICE

PINCH OF CHILLI POWDER

TABBOULEH

8 OZ/225 G BULGHAR WHEAT

1 SMALL RED ONION, FINELY DICED

1 RIPE TOMATO, DE-SEEDED AND FINELY DICED

1 PEACH, STONED AND FINELY DICED

½ SMALL CUCUMBER, PEELED, DE-SEEDED
AND FINELY DICED

2 OZ/50 G CURRANTS

2 TBSP/30 ML CHOPPED FRESH MINT

1 TBSP/15 ML CHOPPED FRESH CORIANDER

DRESSING

4 FLOZ/125 ML VIRGIN OLIVE OIL

JUICE OF 1 LIME

½ TSP/2.5 ML CLEAR HONEY

SALT AND PEPPER

═══

◇ Cut the chicken into thin strips. Heat the oil and stir-fry the strips over a high heat for 2-3 minutes, until browned on all sides. Add the garlic and spices, lower the heat and sauté for 2-3 minutes, until the chicken is cooked through. Remove from the heat and set aside to go cold.
◇ Soak the bulghar in cold water for 15 minutes. Drain well, pressing out as much liquid as possible. Pat dry. Place in a bowl and stir in the remaining ingredients.
◇ Blend the dressing ingredients together and stir ¾ into the salad until evenly combined. Spoon the mixture into 6 lightly oiled 6 floz/175 ml capacity ramekin dishes, pressing firmly, and cover and chill until required.
◇ Remove the moulds from the refrigerator 15 minutes before serving. Unmould onto plates and surround with the spiced chicken, drizzle over the dressing and garnish.

OVEN-BAKED AUBERGINE SALAD

═══

3 SMALL AUBERGINES

SALT

¼ PINT/150 ML VIRGIN OLIVE OIL

1 ONION, THINLY SLICED

1 RED PEPPER, DE-SEEDED AND THINLY SLICED

2 CLOVES GARLIC, CRUSHED

2 BEEF TOMATOES, FINELY CHOPPED

2 TBSP/30 ML CHOPPED FRESH CORIANDER

2 TSP/10 ML PAPRIKA

1 TSP/5 ML GROUND CUMIN

½ TSP/2.5 ML GROUND ALLSPICE

1 TBSP/15 ML LEMON JUICE

4 TBSP/60 ML TOMATO PURÉE

PINCH OF SUGAR

SALT AND PEPPER

═══

◇ Cut a deep slice along the whole length of each aubergine and sprinkle in plenty of salt. Leave to drain.
◇ Heat 3 tbsp/45 ml oil in a frying pan and sauté the onion, pepper and garlic for 10 minutes. Add the tomatoes, coriander, spices, lemon juice, tomato purée, sugar and seasonings and simmer for 5 minutes.
◇ Wash out the aubergines and dry thoroughly. Heat the remaining oil in a large frying pan and fry the aubergines for 5 minutes, until lightly browned on all sides. Remove with a slotted spoon and cool slightly.
◇ Place the aubergines in a baking dish, slit sides up. Carefully prise open the slits and fill with the onion mixture, spooning any extra filling into the dish. Pour in 8 fl oz/225 ml boiling water and bake in a preheated oven at 200°C/400°F/gas mark 6 for 1 hour.
◇ Remove from the oven and leave to go cold. Chill until ready to serve and cut the aubergines into thick slices.
◇ Serve with Greek yogurt and plenty of bread.

LEFT *Spiced chicken with tabbouleh moulds*
RIGHT *Oven-baked aubergine salad*

PORK MEDLEY

~

This stuffed pork fillet is served on a bed of marinated haricot beans and sweet peppers. It is a wonderful medley of flavours, colours and textures, and a mouth-watering supper dish.

2 RED PEPPERS

8 OZ/225 G HARICOT BEANS, SOAKED OVERNIGHT

BOUQUET GARNI

1 CLOVE GARLIC, PEELED

1 TSP/5 ML CUMIN SEEDS

1 TSP/5 ML CORIANDER SEEDS

1 DRIED RED CHILLI, DE-SEEDED

1 BAYLEAF

6 WHOLE PEPPERCORNS

A SMALL PIECE MUSLIN

2×12 OZ/350 G PORK FILLETS

STUFFING

3 APRICOTS, STONED AND FINELY CHOPPED

1 OZ/25 G CASHEW NUTS, TOASTED AND FINELY CHOPPED

1 TBSP/15 ML CHOPPED FRESH SAGE

1 TBSP/15 ML CHOPPED FRESH PARSLEY

PINCH OF GROUND CUMIN

A LITTLE BEATEN EGG TO BIND

DRESSING

¼ PINT/150 ML OLIVE OIL

JUICE OF 2 LEMONS

1 CLOVE GARLIC, CRUSHED

1 TSP/5 ML PAPRIKA

½ TSP/2.5 ML GROUND CUMIN

SALT AND PEPPER

TO GARNISH

LEMON WEDGES

CHOPPED FRESH PARSLEY AND PARSLEY SPRIGS

◇ Place the peppers under a hot grill and cook until the skins are charred and blistered. Tie in a plastic bag and leave until cold.

◇ Drain the soaked beans and place in a large saucepan. Cover with cold water. Tie the bouquet garni ingredients in the muslin and add to the pan. Bring to the boil, boil rapidly for 10 minutes, lower the heat and simmer, uncovered, for 40-45 minutes until the beans are cooked.

◇ Prepare the pork: wash and dry the fillets and split open along 1 side, but do not cut through. Open them out flat and season well. Combine the stuffing ingredients together, adding just enough beaten egg to bind the mixture.

◇ Divide the stuffing between the 2 fillets, spreading it down the centre of each one. Draw the sides of the pork up over the filling and tie firmly with string, at 1 in/2.5 cm intervals, along each fillet.

◇ Place the fillets in a roasting pan and cook in a preheated oven at 200°C/400°F/gas mark 6 for 40 minutes. Remove from the oven and leave until completely cold.

◇ Peel and de-seed the cooked peppers over a bowl to catch any juices. Cut the flesh into thin strips.

◇ Blend the dressing ingredients into the pepper juices.

◇ Drain the cooked beans and discard the bouquet garni. Place in a large bowl and pour in the dressing. Toss well and leave until cold. Stir in the peppers and transfer to a large serving dish.

◇ Remove the string from the cold pork and cut into thick slices. Lay the slices over the marinated beans and peppers and garnish with the lemon wedges, chopped parsley and parsley sprigs.

Pork medley

SALMON & SOLE CEVICHE

~

Adapted from an authentic Samoan recipe, this dish of marinated fish, served with a coconut sauce, is pure delight.

12 OZ/350 G SALMON FILLETS, SKINNED

12 OZ/350 G SOLE FILLETS, SKINNED

MARINADE

JUICE OF 4 LIMES

3 FLOZ/75 ML OLIVE OIL

1 TSP/5 ML SESAME OIL

GRATED RIND OF 2 LIMES

3 INCH/7.5 CM PIECE LEMON GRASS, CRUSHED
OR GRATED RIND OF 1 LEMON

2 SPRING ONIONS, TRIMMED AND
THICKLY SLICED

4 SPRIGS FRESH CORIANDER, BRUISED

1 TSP/5 ML CORIANDER SEEDS, BRUISED

1 SMALL GREEN CHILLI PEPPER, SEEDED
AND SLICED

PINCH OF SUGAR

SAUCE

2 OZ/50 G CREAMED COCONUT

A FEW SHREDDED CORIANDER LEAVES

PINCH OF CAYENNE PEPPER

SALT AND PEPPER

◇ Remove any small bones from the salmon. Slice the salmon and sole fillets thinly, and place in a shallow dish.
◇ Blend together the lime juice, olive oil and sesame oil and pour over the fish. Add the remaining marinade ingredients to the dish, cover and marinate for 2 hours, turning the fish from time to time.
◇ Remove the fish, cover and keep cool. Strain the marinade into a small pan, add the coconut and heat gently, until melted. Remove from the heat and leave to cool.
◇ Stir in the coriander leaves and cayenne and season.
◇ Serve the marinated fish with a spoonful of sauce and a salad garnish.

B.L.T. SALAD

~

Crispy bacon, lettuce and cherry tomatoes make a tasty and attractive salad.

4 OZ/100 G SMOKED BACON, RIND REMOVED

1 OZ/25 G BUTTER

4 SLICES WHITE BREAD, CRUSTS REMOVED
AND CUBED

1 SMALL FRISEE LETTUCE

1 SMALL COS LETTUCE

1 SMALL AVOCADO

6 OZ/175 G MOZZARELLA CHEESE, CUBED

12 CHERRY TOMATOES, HALVED

DRESSING

6 TBSP/90 ML EXTRA VIRGIN OLIVE OIL

2 TBSP/30 ML WHITE WINE VINEGAR

¼ TSP/1.25 ML CHILLI POWDER

SALT

◇ Dice the bacon and stir-fry over a high heat until crisp and golden. Remove with a slotted spoon and drain on kitchen paper.
◇ Add the butter to the pan and stir-fry the cubed bread until crisp and golden. Drain on kitchen paper.
◇ Wash and dry the lettuces, discarding any tough outer leaves and tear into bite-size pieces. Peel, stone and slice the avocado and add to the bowl with the mozzarella and tomatoes.
◇ Blend the dressing ingredients together and pour over the salad. Toss well and serve at once.

FRONT *Salmon and sole ceviche*
BACK *B.L.T. salad*

TIRAMISU WITH RASPBERRIES

~

This is my version of the Italian cream cheese pudding Tiramisu. This recipe serves 8 – 10.

══

ALMOND FINGERS

3 EGGS

3 OZ/75 G SUGAR

2 OZ/50 G GROUND ALMONDS

½ OZ/15 G PLAIN FLOUR

1 OZ/25 G UNSALTED BUTTER, MELTED

8 OZ/225 G RASPBERRIES

¼ PINT/150 ML STRONG BLACK COFFEE

1 TBSP/15 ML BRANDY

3 TBSP/45 ML DARK RUM

12 OZ/350 G MASCARPONE (OR CREAM) CHEESE

1 OZ/25 G SUGAR

2 EGGS, SEPARATED

TOPPING

1 OZ/25 G COCOA POWDER

½ OZ/15 G PLAIN CHOCOLATE, GRATED

══

◇ Beat the eggs and sugar together in a bowl over a pan of simmering water, until thick and pale, about 10 minutes. Fold in the almonds, flour and butter until combined and pour into a greased and lined 9×13 in/23×33 cm Swiss roll tin. Smooth the surface.
◇ Bake in a preheated oven at 190°C/375°F/gas mark 5 for 12-15 minutes, until risen and golden. Turn out and cool on a wire rack. Carefully peel away the baking paper and cut the sponge into 12 large fingers. Place in a large shallow dish and sprinkle over the raspberries.
◇ Mix together the coffee, brandy and 2 tbsp/30 ml of the rum, and pour over the sponge and raspberries.
◇ Beat together the mascarpone, remaining rum, sugar and egg yolks. Whisk the whites until stiff, fold into the mixture and spoon over the sponge. Sift over the cocoa powder, top with grated chocolate and chill for 2 hours.

GINGERBREAD

~

Although this quantity makes a large cake, it keeps very well wrapped in a double layer of foil and stored in a cool place. You'll have no trouble finishing off any leftovers!

══

8 OZ/225 G SOFT BROWN SUGAR

6 OZ/175 G UNSALTED BUTTER

6 OZ/175 G BLACK TREACLE

6 OZ/175 G GOLDEN SYRUP

12 OZ/350 G SELF-RAISING FLOUR

4 OZ/100 G DESICCATED COCONUT

2 TSP/10 ML GROUND GINGER

½ TSP/2.5 ML BICARBONATE OF SODA

½ TSP/2.5 ML SALT

½ PINT/300 ML MILK

1 EGG, LIGHTLY BEATEN

TO SERVE

FRESH APRICOTS

CRÈME FRAÎCHE

══

◇ Grease and line the base and sides of an 8 × 10 in/20 × 25 cm cake tin, or baking tin.
◇ Heat the sugar, butter, treacle and syrup together in a pan, until melted.
◇ Combine the flour, coconut, ginger, bicarbonate of soda and salt in a large bowl. Make a well in the centre and beat in the melted syrup mixture, milk and egg, until combined. Continue to beat for 1 minute.
◇ Pour into the prepared tin and bake in a preheated oven at 180°C/350°F/gas mark 4 for 1¼-1½ hours, or until a skewer inserted in the centre comes out clean.
◇ Cool in the tin for 10 minutes, turn out onto a wire rack and leave to go cold.
◇ Serve cut into fingers with apricots and crème fraîche.

CENTRE AND RIGHT *Tiramisu with raspberries*
LEFT *Gingerbread*

PLUM, SAUTERNES &
CINNAMON ICE-CREAM

~

*Sauternes is a delicious dessert wine making this a
fragrant and refreshingly different ice-cream.*

═══

1 LB/450 G PLUMS

¼ PINT/150 ML SAUTERNES

¾ PINT/450 ML MILK

2 CINNAMON STICKS

6 EGG YOLKS

4 OZ/100 G SUGAR

¼ PINT/150 ML DOUBLE OR WHIPPING CREAM

TO SERVE

3 PLUMS, HALVED, STONED AND SLICED

A LITTLE EXTRA SAUTERNES (OPTIONAL)

═══

◇ Halve and stone the plums and place in a saucepan.
Add the Sauternes and bring to the boil, cover and simmer
gently for 5 minutes, until the plums are soft. Purée until
smooth and leave to go cold.
◇ Scald the milk with the cinnamon, infuse for 10
minutes, and strain.
◇ Beat the egg yolks and sugar together until pale and
creamy, pour in the milk, beating all the time, and strain
through a fine sieve into a clean pan. Heat gently, stirring,
until the mixture thickens and coats the back of the spoon.
Do not let the custard boil or it will curdle. Remove from
the heat and leave to go cold.
◇ Combine the fruit purée and custard. Lightly whip the
cream and fold into the mixture. Place in a plastic container and transfer to the freezer.
◇ Freeze for 3-4 hours, beating well every hour or so to
prevent ice crystals forming.
◇ Remove the ice-cream from the freezer 15 minutes
before serving, to allow it to soften slightly. Scoop into
dishes and serve topped with fresh plum slices and a little
Sauternes, if liked.

SPICED BRAISED
PEARS

~

*In this refreshing and light summer dessert the pears
are braised with red wine, port and spices and served
chilled, with ice-cream or cream.*

═══

6 OZ/175 G SUGAR

7 FLOZ/200 ML DRY RED WINE

¼ PINT/150 ML WATER

2 TBSP/30 ML PORT

4 STRIPS LEMON PEEL

JUICE OF 1 LEMON

2 CINNAMON STICKS

6 WHOLE CLOVES

6 MEDIUM DESSERT PEARS

TO SERVE

VANILLA ICE-CREAM

WHIPPED CREAM

═══

◇ Place all the ingredients, except the pears, in a large
pan. Heat gently until the sugar is dissolved.
◇ Peel the pears leaving the stalk in place and add to the
pan. Bring the liquid just to boiling point, cover and simmer over a very low heat for 35-40 minutes, turning the
pears frequently. Do not allow the liquid to boil or the
pears will become mushy.
◇ Transfer the pears to a serving dish and pour over the
liquid. Leave to go cold and refrigerate until well chilled.
◇ Serve the pears with ice-cream or whipped cream,
whichever you prefer.

RIGHT *Plum, Sauternes and cinnamon ice-cream*
LEFT *Spiced braised pears*

CITRUS ICE-CREAM SHERBET

~

Freshly squeezed grapefruit and orange juice is served with a scoop of vanilla ice-cream, and topped up with soda water, for a delicious non-alcoholic fruit sherbet.

═══

¾ PINT/450 ML FRESHLY SQUEEZED
GRAPEFRUIT JUICE

¾ PINT/450 ML FRESHLY SQUEEZED
ORANGE JUICE

6 SCOOPS VANILLA ICE-CREAM

¾ PINT/450 ML CHILLED SODA WATER

═══

◇ Blend the fruit juices together and pour into 6 large tumblers.

◇ Add a scoop of ice-cream to each glass, top up with the soda water and serve immediately.

ICED MOCHA COFFEE

~

A deliciously rich chocolate-flavoured iced coffee – perfect for a hot summer day. This drink should be served as chilled as possible.

═══

1½ PINT/900 ML BOILING WATER

2 OZ/50 G GROUND MEDIUM ROAST COFFEE

3 OZ/75 G PLAIN CHOCOLATE, GRATED

1½-2 OZ/40-50 G SUGAR

TO SERVE

MILK OR SINGLE CREAM

═══

◇ Pour the boiling water over the coffee in a cafetière or large heat-proof jug and allow to infuse for 10 minutes.

◇ Either plunge the stopper or pour the coffee through a fine sieve and stir in the chocolate and sugar until dissolved. Leave to cool and refrigerate for several hours or overnight.

◇ Remove from the refrigerator just before serving, stir well and pass through a fine sieve.

◇ Divide between 6 large tumblers and top up with the milk or cream to taste.

CHAMPAGNE SUNSET

~

This delicious champagne cocktail is loosely based on a tequila sunrise. It makes the perfect aperitif for a warm summer evening.

═══

½ PINT/300 ML FRESHLY SQUEEZED
ORANGE JUICE

6 TBSP/90 ML COINTREAU

1×75 CL BOTTLE CHILLED CHAMPAGNE

GRENADINE

═══

◇ Blend the orange juice and Cointreau together and divide between 6 champagne flutes.

◇ Top up with champagne, add a dash of grenadine to each glass and serve immediately.

BACK LEFT *Citrus ice-cream sherbet*
FRONT *Iced mocha coffee*
BACK RIGHT *Champagne sunset*

~

I N D E X

ACKNOWLEDGMENTS

~

The publishers would like to thank the following for
their help in the preparation of this book:

Alison Leach for the index

Mary Talbot for use of The Old Farm

For picnicware and fabrics:

Brats Ltd
281 King's Road
London SW3

Ian Mankin Ltd
109 Regent's Park Road
London NW1

Antoinette Putnam
55 Regent's Park Road
London NW1